Handy Homes for Creepy Crawlies

Also by Margaret Crush from Granada
in hardback

What's in our World?

Margaret Crush

HANDY HOMES FOR CREEPY CRAWLIES

Illustrated by Sally Kindberg

A DRAGON BOOK

GRANADA

London Toronto Sydney New York

Published by Granada Publishing Limited in 1982

ISBN 0 583 30484 2

Copyright © Margaret Crush 1982

Granada Publishing Limited
Frogmore, St Albans, Herts AL2 2NF
and
36 Golden Square, London W1R 4AH
866 United Nations Plaza, New York, NY 10017, USA
117 York Street, Sydney, NSW 2000, Australia
100 Skyway Avenue, Rexdale, Ontario, M9W 3A6, Canada
61 Beach Road, Auckland, New Zealand

Printed and bound in Great Britain by
Cox & Wyman Ltd, Reading, Berks.
Set in Times

Granada ®
Granada Publishing ®

Contents

Grateful thanks are due to Alfred Leutscher, formerly Education Officer at the Natural History Museum, to David R. Ragge, of the Department of Entomology, and to Michael Chinery, for kindly reading the manuscript and making helpful suggestions.

Introduction

Cats and dogs, rabbits and guinea pigs, hamsters, gerbils and so on are popular pets. Many people keep them, and get great fun and pleasure from them. But these domestic pets can be expensive to buy. Even if you are lucky enough to be given one, it can be quite costly to feed. And many are not for people who live in flats or houses without gardens.

If you do live in a flat, or a house without a garden, it doesn't mean you cannot keep a pet at all. Look around you in the garden, park or countryside, and you will find many fascinating, so-called 'creepy crawlies' that will make unusual pets, ones that you can keep in a small space, without too much expense. Or, you may come across such a mini-beast by accident and want to keep it for a while to watch it and see how it behaves. If you are not sure what you have found, there is a list of useful books at the end of the book. Most of the creepy crawlies in this book live naturally in this country, but there are also a few foreign ones (such as stick insects and silkworms) which you can buy very cheaply. As well as actual creepy crawlies, the book also covers other 'found' pets ('pets for free', we could call them), such as grass snakes, lizards, tadpoles and newts – all interesting good fun to keep.

Each chapter gives some suggestions on how to keep some of these creatures as pets. Remember, though – the suggestions are just that – *suggestions*! Pet-keeping, especially of such unusual creatures, is a vast subject. The longer you keep any pet, the more you find out about it. You may find out a hitherto unknown fact or discover a problem that the book doesn't cover. Indeed, you may well be the first person to have this particular problem! However, most things can be solved if you find out as much about your pets as you can, not only from this book but others in the library, from films and television programmes. If none of these answers your questions, try the appropriate keeper (i.e. the insect keeper or the reptile keeper) at your nearest zoo, or try the appropriate department at a college or university.

Many of these 'creepy crawly' pets are for watching only, not for stroking like a kitten nor picking up like a hamster. However, they all need just as much care. You should never neglect any living creature – and especially not if it's small and mute and can't tell you its needs. Never think just because something's an insect that it doesn't need proper food and housing, nor to be kept clean. Remember, an insect has likes and dislikes just as you do. If it's not looked after properly, it won't be happy and you will have been unkind to remove it from its natural surroundings. Any creature removed from its proper environment and imprisoned in a cage is *totally* dependent on its keeper for its well being, and must be looked after every single day.

All this may sound rather boring, but feeding and cleaning are jobs you must do every day, whether you feel like it or not. Imagine if you got no meals for a day because no one felt like preparing them – and you were locked up in your room, so you couldn't forage for yourself! Anyone who thinks they couldn't look after a pet as regularly as this, really shouldn't keep one.

Other things to remember when keeping any pet is to be very particular about cleanliness when handling it or looking after it in any way. Wash your hands *beforehand* for its sake, and *afterwards* for yours!

Another vital item is a secure cage. This book gives you some ideas for simple 'homes' you can make, often from things you have around the house. It is very important that your pets do not escape, especially if they are 'creepy crawlies'. Often other people, especially some grown-ups, don't feel the same way as you do about creepy crawlies. They may actually be frightened of them, or they may just think them dirty, unhygienic or destructive. Nothing will turn grown-ups off your keeping a creepy crawly quicker than finding it in the larder, crawling over the bed, or leering at them from the bath!

So, good 'public relations' are essential. Reassure people that your pet won't escape from its home, and then *make sure* it doesn't. Also, never try to frighten people with your pet. Many people are irrationally but genuinely terrified of spiders. If you are lucky enough to like these leggy beasts and keep one as a pet, then don't use it to tease the spider-haters.

If by any mischance you are absolutely forbidden to keep any pet, Chapter 18 on 'liberty' pets, that is wild animals that live in your garden and can be encouraged by you, has been written especially with you in mind. Or, of course, you could keep a 'pet rock' or even a Venus Fly Trap a plant that seems almost alive!

One final thing – do try to preserve wild life as much as you can. Don't be greedy when collecting specimens – and don't take every example of a particular species you may see in one spot. Also, some creatures – and plants too – are rare or even protected by law. Check you have not found one of these. If you have, leave it where you found it, so it has a chance to reproduce and – you hope – continue its species.

All this may seem like rather a lot of 'don'ts', but the rules are really very simple. Look after your pet properly, feed it, clean it, and keep it secure – and you'll have enormous fun. Perhaps you will even develop a lifelong interest in it so you want to study creepy crawlies as a career. In which case, so much the better – and the best of luck!

1

Rearing caterpillars and chrysalises

Caterpillars are perhaps the commonest creepy-crawlies that people keep. Like tadpoles, they make an amazing change into their grown-up stage. The wriggly, many-legged, earthbound caterpillar changes first into a legless, motionless pupa (also called a chrysalis). It then changes again inside the pupa to emerge as a fully grown, airborne butterfly or moth, with incredibly beautiful wings, and six legs.

Often, when you find a caterpillar, and more especially a pupa, it's difficult to tell to which family of butterflies or moths it belongs. It's therefore good fun to make a home for it so you can keep it just until it emerges as an adult insect. At that point you should let it go, especially as butterflies are getting more and more scarce these days. It can then lay its eggs, and the whole life cycle will start over again.

Here are a couple of 'caterpillar farms' you can make quite easily. For the first one, get an old metal cake tin, or the sort of round tin some ground coffee comes in. If it has a lid, bang some air holes in it with a hammer and a biggish nail. (A helpful grown-up or handy older brother or sister might help with this.) Remember it's sensible to ask if you can take something before you gaily abscond from home with it. You'll be much more

11

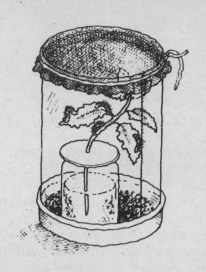

make sure your
pets do not escape

Caterpillar farms

popular if you ask permission to use it – and, if you're lucky, may even get help setting up your 'farm'!

Get some clear acetate (you can buy this from an art shop). Cut a piece about 45 cm high and 1 cm wider than the circumference of the tin. Look at the top picture opposite. So you don't buy more than you need, tie a bit of string round the tin and measure how long it is. Bend the acetate into a cylinder shape inside the base of the tin, so it just fits, and staple or stick the edges together with strong glue. If the tin has a lid use it – with holes punctured in it – for the top of' the acetate. If it hasn't cut a piece of old nylon tights, muslin or cheesecloth to fit over the top and tie on with string or a big elastic band.

The other very easy kind of farm is made from a large grocery carton. Look at the bottom picture opposite. Cut out panels from the sides, top and front, and cover them with muslin, cheesecloth, or the sort of net dressmakers use. Do make sure the edges of the material are firmly stuck down, because caterpillars are great escape artistes. If the box doesn't have a lid of its own, cover the top with a piece of net tied on firmly with string.

Before installing your caterpillar, put a layer of peat or gardener's compost an inch or so thick in the bottom of the tin or box, and sink a small jar (a paste pot or a small mustard-type jar will do) in it. Fill the jar with water and place the food plant in it. Plug the neck of the plant holder jar with tissue paper or a cardboard disc, so the caterpillar doesn't fall in the water and drown. Don't stand the cage in the sun because condensation will form on the inside.

Now hunt for a caterpillar! Good places to look are hedges, stinging nettle patches and flower beds. Clues to look for are holes nibbled in leaves, especially in

Lifting caterpillars on paint brush

your cabbages. Collect the caterpillar carefully, or you may squash it. A good way is to put an old teaspoon alongside each mini-caterpillar. With *very* gentle pushing it will eventually roll on to the teaspoon. If it is very small, a paintbrush is much better than a finger. Never handle caterpillars with your fingers, and that goes for butterflies and moths, too, because you may damage them. If for some reason you must pick a butterfly up, use your cupped hands very gently.

Pick up some of the plant the caterpillars are on. This is called the food plant and it should be put in the pot in the farm. Take the caterpillar home in a small box or jar with air holes. Put the food plant in the little jar of water to keep it fresh, and put the caterpillar on the plant. Make sure the plant is touching one wall of the cage, so if the caterpillar gets on to the floor it can climb up the wall and back on to the plant. When the caterpillar has eaten all the leaves of the food plant, or when they start to wilt, replace them with fresh ones from the same kind of plant. Incidentally, don't overcrowd the caterpillars – two or three in a farm are enough. And don't mix up different kinds, especially not hairy caterpillars with smooth ones.

Keep your farm in a light place, but not in direct sun. Every day, take out dead leaves and any waste the caterpillar has made, and replace the food plant and water as necessary. If you stand fresh food beside the old for a little while, the caterpillars will probably transfer to it.

If your caterpillar is fairly young, it will change its skin several times when the old one gets too tight, growing each time. The caterpillar will make a pad of silk to which it will cling for several days, staying motionless while the skin change is happening. Sometimes you may have to remove dead caterpillars from the farm, but be careful that you don't remove any which are only having a skin change. You should also be careful that you do not detach them from their silken pads.

Eventually, the caterpillar will pupate to rest for a while. Just before this, it may be rather fidgety, crawling around a lot. If you have too many caterpillars in your farm, they may disturb each other at this stage, and may not pupate correctly. So put some in a separate cage.

A moth caterpillar will most likely pupate in the soil, and a butterfly caterpillar on the netting or plants. You could add a few twigs in case it prefers these, but don't cram in so many that it can't find a place to spin. If your farm is the cardboard box type, you could put in a plastic container of soil. The change to a pupa usually takes three to four days. Sometimes you find a pupa in the garden – keep it in the same way, and you will have great fun seeing what hatches out.

Unless your pupa is one that doesn't need to overwinter before hatching in the spring, it's best to leave it where it is in the farm. The adult should hatch two to three weeks later. If the weather is hot and dry, occasionally spray the pupa gently with water. If the pupa needs to be stored for the winter, move it carefully, with the twig it is on, into an airtight tin in tissue paper, and leave it in a cool place like an outhouse. Pupae need little or no air, and the closed atmosphere prevents them drying up. Open the tin occasionally, and sprinkle in a few drops of tepid water, or breathe on the pupa a few times, to give a bit of moisture. About three weeks before the creature is due to emerge (check this with a butterfly or moth identification book), open up the dormitory tin, and pop the pupa into the farm again. Preferably this should be the box type farm, as the first type has sides rather too slippery for the emerging insect. Make sure there are plenty of twigs or netting for the creature to climb up to dry its wings. Spray the pupa daily with a fine spray until the butterfly emerges.

It's not always possible to be around to see the caterpillar pupate, or the butterfly or moth struggle out of its pupa. If you *are* lucky enough to see this, it's something you'll never forget. Sometimes you may be unlucky and hatch out a parasitic fly or wasp which laid its eggs in the caterpillar or the pupa.

At the other end of the life cycle, you may be lucky enough to see a butterfly or moth laying its eggs. Then you can pick a *small* part of the plant with not more

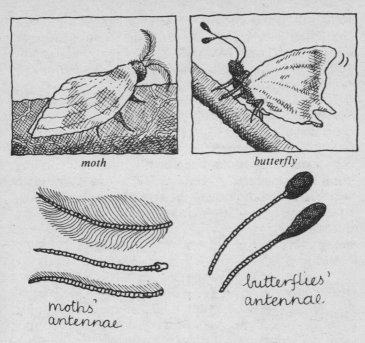

moths' antennae

butterflies' antennae.

Differences between moths and butterflies

than a dozen eggs on, take it home and try to rear the young. Don't take any more as some butterflies really *are* very scarce these days and some species are actually in danger of dying out. The Large Blue butterfly became extinct in England as recently as 1979. Because many butterflies are becoming scarce it is not a good idea for you to keep adult insects. Although moths are more common (97 per cent of all of the order Lepidoptera are moths and only 3 per cent are butterflies) you can't always tell whose eggs you have collected. If you see the adult insects it is very easy to tell them apart, as you can see in the illustration. Moths fold their wings flat on their backs when at rest but butterflies rest with their wings held close together above their bodies. Also, if you can get close enough, you will see that moths' antennae have either feathery, pointed or blunted ends, and butterflies' antennae have thickened ends.

Put the eggs in a small plastic box, out of the sun, until they hatch. They may darken a bit just before this. When the tiny caterpillars hatch out, they are best kept in a 'caterpillar crèche' for a little while before putting them in the big farm. A sandwich box about 18 x 12 x 5 cm will do for the crèche. Line it with paper and provide some fresh cuttings of the food plant. Change

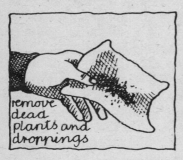

Cleaning out caterpillar farm

the paper liner and food every day, but don't move the mini-caterpillars from the food they are on. Cut round it and put it and them in with the fresh plant. Look at the illustration to see exactly how to do it. Keep the box out of the sun. When the caterpillars get bigger, you can transfer them to the big farm.

To study an adult insect, you could perhaps keep a moth for a little while. There are several ways of catching moths. You can go to scented flowers at dusk, and catch the moths with a net. (You can see how to make one on page 21.) Don't make the sweeps of the net too violent, though, or you'll hurt the creatures. Perhaps a better method if the moth settles is to use the jam jar and card technique. On page 58 there is a drawing showing how to catch creatures using this method.

You can attract moths to a light, either in a porch, or indoors if you leave a window open. If you have a properly insulated, outdoor light bulb on a very long lead, or a Calor gas camping lamp, you can put this in the garden. Hang a white sheet near the lamp, so that the light falls on it. The moths will be fascinated by the light and settle on the sheet. (Make sure the lamp doesn't touch the sheet, though, or you may have an unintentional bonfire!)

Another way of attracting moths is called sugaring. Mix up some sweet stuff – beer and brown sugar or treacle is a good recipe. The beery smell will attract them to settle and the sweet ingredients will keep them there. Paint it at nose height on several tree trunks or posts at dusk. Usually nothing much will happen on the first evening. Then, depending on the weather and the mixture, enraptured and drunken moths should cluster round. If they don't, come back in half an hour or so – and, if you still haven't caught anything, try on

Light trap

successive evenings.

To keep your moths for a little while to examine them, you'll need a cage which gives them room to flutter about.

The cardboard box type of caterpillar farm will do well. You'll have to keep it out of the sun and give it a *fine* spray of tepid water in hot weather. However, as your moths will need their own natural food plant, and you may have difficulty supplying this, it's probably much easier to keep them only a few hours to look at, and to concentrate on keeping caterpillars and pupae.

Really the best thing you can do for adult butterflies and moths is to attract them to your garden. Persuade whoever does the planting to leave one corner as a butterfly garden. Leave the grass unmown and don't weed out nettles, ragwort, dandelions, clover and thistles! If possible, grow garden plants attractive to butterflies. Plant a buddleia – also called the Butterfly

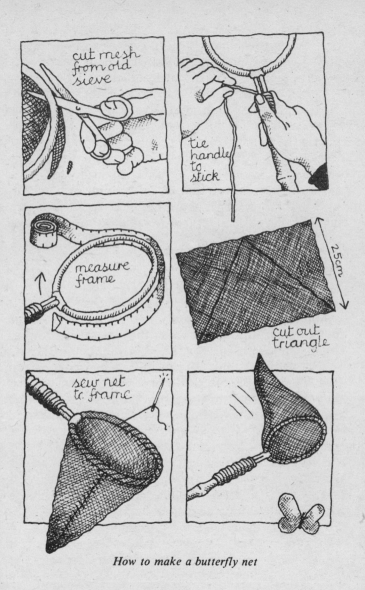

How to make a butterfly net

Bush. If you've ever seen one, you'll know why it has been given this name. Butterflies such as the Peacock and, if you are lucky, the Red Admiral, will settle on its flowers, sipping their nectar in ecstasy.

Other plants which will encourage butterflies and other insects to your garden are aubretia, choisya (Mexican orange bush), lavender, sweet rocket, ice plant, fruit trees (for their flowers), helianthemums (rock roses), honeysuckle, Michaelmas daisies, night-scented stock and tobacco plants (especially for moths at dusk), potentilla, thyme, viburnum, golden rod, wallflowers, sweet william and candytuft. Also plant ivy and periwinkle to provide resting spots and cover for insects at night.

Some butterflies hibernate in odd corners in attics, sheds and similar places. On a sunny winter's day, you may be upset to find a butterfly (especially a Small Tortoiseshell) beating its wings feebly against a window pane. You decide to let it out in the open air. Well, in fact, that is just about the *worst* thing you can do, for it won't survive the cold nights. It may die indoors anyway, but you can try to help it, by offering it some syrup dissolved in warm water. Then let it go back to its corner for the rest of the winter – and hope for the best!

2

Making an ant farm

Ants are called social insects – they live like hive bees in communities, each ant having a special job to do. Each worker ant is responsible for something – collecting food, looking after the eggs laid by the queen ant, caring for the larvae they hatch into, constructing, repairing or guarding the nest. The worker ants are all females, but only the queen ant lays eggs. Male ants do no work at all. Their only function is to mate with the queen.

There are many thousands of ant species in the world. Of the forty-seven British kinds, the ones you keep will depend very much on where you live. There are six common kinds, and you may very well find the Black ant in your garden. The largest British ants (about 1 cm long) are called Wood ants. They build huge nests of pine needles and twigs, 60 to 90 cm high. These ants are *not* suitable for keeping in an ant palace as they squirt formic acid on to the glass and make it smeary and difficult to see through.

A few specialized shops and mail order firms will sell you an ant palace (also called a *formicarium* after the Latin word for 'ant'). Such a palace is usually made of two pieces of clear plastic or glass stuck together in a narrow box shape so you can see the ants soldiering away.

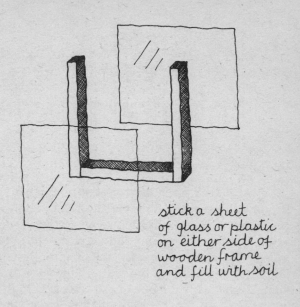

stick a sheet
of glass or plastic
on either side of
wooden frame
and fill with soil

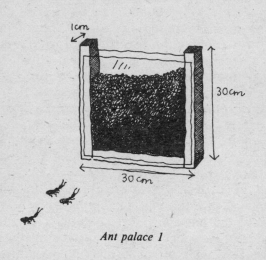

1cm

30cm

30 cm

Ant palace 1

make a moat
to keep ants
in your palace

Ant Palace 3

It's much cheaper, more fun, and not too difficult to build your own ant palace. If you're not too confident about making things, perhaps a grown-up or older brother or sister will give you a hand.

You can construct a palace similar to the bought ones, by using two pieces of clear plastic sheet about 30 cms square, and three bits of wood stuck together with strong glue (quick-drying waterproof resin is good). Fill the palace with fine soil to within 2 cm of the top.

Another way of making an ant palace is to use an ordinary strong garden seedbox. Line the sides and bottom with polythene sheeting, trimming off the

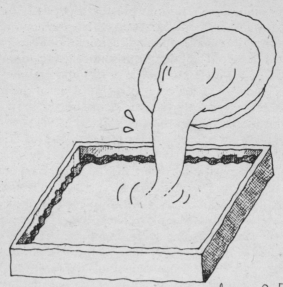

leave 2.5 cm
gap for nest
area entrance

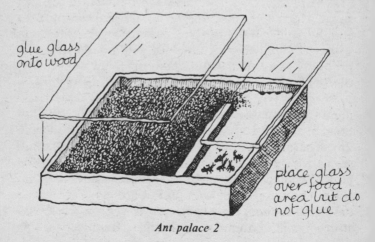

glue glass
onto wood

place glass
over food
area but do
not glue

Ant palace 2

26

surplus material. Get some plaster of Paris (from a chemist or model shop). Mix it up with water according to the directions on the packet, using an old washing-up bowl and old spoon. Pour the mixture into the seedbox so it flows into all the nooks and crannies of the polythene. Fill the tray to within 2 cm of the top, push a piece of wood (about 2 cm shorter than the width of the tray) into the wet plaster. Make sure the top of the wood is level with the top of the tray. Look at the pictures.

When the plaster has dried, fill the larger part of the box with fine soil, and stick a glass cover on it. Cover the smaller part of the box with a piece of removable glass. (If you have any plaster left over, don't put it down the sink because it will bung it up! Let it set in a disposable container and put it all in the dustbin.)

Perhaps the easiest ant palace of all is a large 2 lb coffee jar or similar glass container, with a smaller jar or container nesting inside it. Keep the lid on the smaller one, and use it as the ants' 'dining table'. (Those plastic 'nesting' storage containers for tea and sugar which come in round or square shapes would do equally well.) Fill the space between the containers with soil – and there is a palace with no construction problems at all. You should put only a few ants in this, though.

Both this type of ant palace and the upright kind first mentioned need to stand in a dish or old washing-up bowl of water, as a sort of moat (see the picture on page 25). The moat will keep the ants *in* their palace and stop them rampaging round your kitchen looking for jam. Put a few drops of detergent on the surface of the water, because small ants can walk on water! The detergent reduces the surface tension of the water and stops the ants marching over it. (For extra safety, if you like, you can put a cover on the top of the palace. If it has a moat, this isn't strictly necessary, but it might be a prudent 'public relations' thing to do. If people aren't too keen on your keeping ants, the cover makes the whole thing *look* more secure!)

Punch lots of very small holes in the lid of a screwtop jam jar – then off you go ant-hunting! You can often locate a nest by spotting lots of ants scurrying around a particular spot, or by seeing a raised-up bit of earth with lots of extra tiny particles of soil. This is the roof of the nest. Alternatively, you could turn over a number of biggish stones, and you should find ants bustling about. Collect as many as you can, and also some grubs and cocoons. People often wrongly call these cocoons 'ant's eggs' – they are the ones often fed to goldfish. They are not eggs, however, but the ants' pupae – the same stage in an ant's life as a chrysalis is in a butterfly's.

You may have to dig gently into the nest for the grubs and pupae and the worker ants will no doubt rush madly about, swarming over your fingers and trying desperately to shift their young. Always pick them up carefully, with a paintbrush (see page 14). Sometimes you will be lucky and find the young at the surface under a flat stone (ants like a roof to their nest). If you can get the queen – you can easily recognize her because she will be much larger than the others and probably near the centre of the nest – your palace really *will* be a palace. Without a queen the colony will not function properly, although workers will live a long time. To increase your chances, put a piece of thin plastic or slate (through which the warmth of the sun will pass more easily) in place of the stone covering a nest. Come back after a day or so, pick up the 'solar' roof, and you may find the ants have come near the surface with some of their young – and with luck a queen.

Carry the ants home in your collecting jar with some soil. Put them on top of the earth in the palace. If you cover them do leave a way in for air; if you don't, don't forget the moat! If they have neither moat nor cover, they may raid the larder – and you will be unpopular!

Ants have an extremely keen sense of smell. There was once an ants' nest outside my front door. The ants managed to infiltrate a crack in the door and tracked 6 metres or so through the hall, into the kitchen, up a working unit, and into the jam cupboard. For days afterwards, the hall had a constant stream of ants passing and repassing – all along *exactly* the same track! From which you can guess that when ants find what they like to eat best the message travels back quickly to the nest. So feed your colony on sugar, bits of jam, honey mixed with water, and so on. The ants will also enjoy pieces of cooked meat, dead insects, bird seed, fish food, breadcrumbs – indeed, almost any food scraps. Melted butter and raw egg white will help give them a balanced diet. They will drag the food down into their burrows to eat or store. Keep the surface of the earth moist to provide water for your pets, or put in a small sponge and keep it damp.

Keep the palace in darkness for a day or so. Ants prefer the dark, but do not mind red light. You can occasionally use a red light bulb, or a piece of red cellophane (perhaps from a chocolate box) fixed over a torch bulb with a rubber band. The ants should then soldier away near the walls where you can watch them tunnelling and working.

Some people keep an ant colony going for years. In the wild colonies have been known to survive for 20 years or so. For you, it's probably best and more public-spirited to let your ants go just before 'flying time' – July or August. Empty the ants and soil out together into the garden. Then next spring, if you want to, collect some more and start a new colony.

3

Keeping earwigs and woodlice

The female earwig is one of the best mothers in the insect world. She looks after her clutch of 40 to 60 tiny oval white eggs, constantly licking them and turning them over. If she thinks they're in danger, she carries them away one by one to a safer place. Unlike most other insects who ignore both eggs and young, the earwig feeds and protects her hatchlings until they can fend for themselves.

It is also surprising to some people that an earwig is an insect, but it has all the correct insect characteristics – head, thorax and abdomen, and six legs. Like beetles, the common British earwig has two hard wingcases which usually cover two transparent wings – though it hardly ever flies. At the end of its body it has pincers which can nip. Earwigs are about 2 cm long, and can be found all the year round, but especially in summer. They are very fond of chrysanthemums and dahlias. To catch earwigs, gardeners often put an upside-down flower pot, filled with paper, on top of a dahlia stake, and the earwigs lurk in it.

The best time to find a female earwig with a family is in February and March – if you turn over largish stones and old logs, you may find her hovering over her eggs or young. The young are pale versions of their parents.

They moult several times, growing larger after each shedding of their skins.

If you decide to take the family home to study them for a little while, try not to disturb the mother more than necessary. She is so solicitous that she might decide the only way to protect her young is to eat them! (Unfortunately, she may also do this if you don't feed her enough protein.) One of the best ways of collecting earwigs is to pick up mother, eggs or young, and what they are resting on (earth, leaves or whatever) with an old spoon.

The best home for earwigs is a small plastic box or glass tube such as you get in a chemistry lab. Make sure air can get in, but keep a lid on. If the home is made of glass, cover it up when you're not feeding the family. When you want to look at them, do so for only a short time, as earwigs don't like too much light. They are scavengers by nature, and will eat various things, especially enjoying freshly killed flies. (Make sure the flies are not ones you've blasted with flykiller, though, or you'll poison your pet.) Earwigs also eat scraps of vegetables. If you put a few drops of water in their container, it will be both a drink and a way of keeping the atmosphere slightly moist.

Even scientists don't know all there is to know about earwigs. If you keep careful notes on what you observe, especially anything unusual, you may find out something that even the entomologists didn't know!

Another creepy crawly interesting to keep for a while is a woodlouse. Woodlice are not insects nor, of course, for the benefit of anxious enquirers in your family, are they lice! If you check the number of their legs, you can confirm they are not insects – they have seven pairs of legs. They are, in fact, members of the crustacean family, as are crabs, shrimps and lobsters. They have a segmented body protected by tough plates. The female has a little pouch under her body for eggs. There are about thirty native species – the one that rolls into a ball when prodded is called the armadillo or pill woodlouse.

Woodlouse home

You will often find woodlice in the same sort of places as earwigs – under stones in damp spots. They loathe the light and you must never let them dry out, or they will be unable to breathe. The best home for them is an old aquarium or one of those plastic stacking cake tins, with a sheet of glass or clear plastic on top to stop them clambering out. Raise this *very slightly* on matchsticks or lumps of modelling clay to let some air in. Cover the floor of their home with damp peat, and make sure that it remains damp.

Put in a lump of damp and rotting wood. The more revolting it looks, the better the woodlice will like it. You'll probably find a suitable chunk where you found the woodlice; if not, look in a shady woodland area. Your woodlice will want to hide from the light, so keep their home covered when you are not looking after – or at – them. Give them bits of old carrot, potato and lettuce stalks as well as the rotten wood.

4

Rearing silkworms

Most of the pets in this book can support themselves perfectly well and successfully in the wild. The subjects of this chapter have been reared by humans for so many thousands of years that they are now completely dependent on them. Their caterpillars will not search for food, and their moths cannot feed. They cannot fly, even when they are in danger. They are kept for the wonderful material they spin in their transformation from caterpillar to moth.

You've guessed! The creature is the silkworm which produces the strong, shining thread we call silk. Silkworms were reared by the Chinese over 5,000 years ago. So precious was the silk they produced that its origin was kept a closely guarded secret. Anyone who told an outsider that it came from a tiny worm would be punished by death. There are various stories of how the secret was finally let out and some silkworm eggs smuggled to the West. One tells of a princess who hid some of the eggs in her headdress when she left China to marry an Indian prince. Fortunately, nobody suspected her plan, or even she would have been sentenced to death.

Today, silkworms are reared in several countries, including Italy, France, Britain, China, and Japan which has a climate especially suitable for growing the silkworms' food plant, the mulberry tree. Silkworms really like only mulberry leaves. If they haven't ever tasted mulberry or are really, *really* hungry, they will condescend to nibble lettuce. This will keep them alive, but they may not complete their life cycle nor spin silk. So, unless you have access to a mulberry tree whose leaves you are allowed to pick regularly, keeping silkworms is not for you.

Silkworms are the caterpillars of the silk moth and they pass through the same stages as the young of other moths, that is caterpillar (or larva), pupa and adult (moth). Each female moth lays several hundred tiny white eggs, the size of a mustard seed. There are over 1,000 of them to a gramme! The best way of getting eggs is for another silkworm-keeper to give you some, but you can sometimes buy them in specialized pet shops, or by mail order.

The eggs must be kept warm indoors. You can keep your silkworms in a caterpillar farm, or, as is done in commercial breeding, on a tray covered with cheesecloth. Three to ten days after being laid, they should hatch out into tiny caterpillars about 3 mm long. Usually the hatching takes place in the early morning. The cheesecloth will provide something for the tiny worms to crawl through leaving their egg cases behind. A silkworm is really just a moving mouth! It has the equivalent of a heart, but no other blood vessels, or lungs. It breathes from holes along its sides. It is born voraciously hungry; day and night it never stops eating. For your silkworm's first feed, cover the tray with some tender young mulberry leaves, chopped up.

Don't try to pick the worms up, as they are easily damaged. To transfer them to a rearing tray, let them crawl on to the chopped leaves, and then move the leaves to the second tray. The worms are so enraptured with their food you won't need a cover on them until they're ready to spin their cocoons, about a month later.

Before this, they will moult (split their skins) four times, and grow *enormously*. Their weight increases 10,000 times. It is as if a 4 kilo baby grew up to weigh 40,000 kilos! So, if you have a lot of worms, you'll need to give them more room as they grow, by transferring some of them to extra trays.

The ideal temperature to keep them in is 18 to 25 degrees Centigrade. If it is any cooler they may die of cold; any hotter, and they will die of heat! They need fresh air, but not a breeze or draught. (When reared commercially, they have air-conditioning!) Once a day you must clean them out. Wash your hands beforehand for the worms' sakes – and afterwards for yours! To do the cleaning – or indeed to move them to bigger and better trays at any time – the easiest thing is to put an old net curtain or similar piece of holey material covered with mulberry leaves over the tray. The worms will push eagerly through the mesh to get at the fresher leaves, and you can transfer the net, leaves, worms and all to a clean tray.

From about 20 days after hatching, watch your worms carefully. When they stop eating and start waving their heads about, they are ready to spin their silk and make the cocoons inside which they will change into pupae and then into moths. Shift them carefully into a cardboard box with twigs, eggboxes or a loose bundle of straw inside. They will spin their cocoons on the twigs or inside the eggboxes. After 24 hours the worm will have covered itself with the cocoon and disappeared, but it goes on spinning inside for another three to five days – until it has forced out the last drop of silk-making liquid from the two sacs on either side of its body. While it is spinning, you should take care it is not disturbed, especially by noise, as it may stop spinning or break its thread. Inside its cocoon it moults for the last time and becomes a pupa.

After two weeks as a pupa, the insect will struggle free as a moth. Usually, moths emerge in the early morning. The females give off a special scent to attract a male who then whirrs his wings furiously in a courting dance. After the mating, the male dies off in a couple of days, but the female becomes very busy. She starts laying eggs a few hours after mating and continues for two days. The eggs are laid in neat rows on mulberry leaves, or on paper or card if you provide her with these. It is then quite easy to put the eggs and the paper on a hatching tray. Her eggs laid, the silkworm moth's lifework is done, and very soon she dies.

You may want to try your hand at spinning off some silk. But to do that, you will have to sacrifice some of your potential moths, by killing the pupa. Rub the silky fuzz off some of the cocoons with your fingers, and put them in the oven at the highest temperature for half an hour. Then boil the cocoons in water for about 10 minutes to soften them, and the loose ends of silk should float free. Be careful not to scald yourself!

Wrap the loose end round a pencil and start winding it off. It takes rather a lot of winding before the silk on the pencil actually becomes visible. There is about half a mile of silk on a cocoon! Commercially, of course, this process is carried out by machine. Just imagine how many cocoons you'd have to unwind to make a silk dress or even a silk tie!

5

Keeping stick insects

Most people think of stick insects as the kind you can buy very cheaply in pet shops – long-bodied insects with right-angled legs, beautifully camouflaged against the green twigs and leaves to which they cling. Stick insects are also called 'walking sticks'. Most kinds live in the Far East, although some are found in Southern Europe and North America, and a few have naturalized themselves in greenhouses in Britain.

To keep stick insects, whether bought or found by accident, you need a small jar for the food plant and a small fish tank or a tall large jar for your 'stickery'. This must be at least twice as high as the insects are long. Cover it with a lid of some kind, but this must have lots of airholes in it. Perforated zinc or *very fine* meshed netting or cheesecloth are good. Put a layer of peat about 2·5 cm thick in the bottom and add a supply of leafy twigs for perches. Naturalized British stick insects will eat privet, ivy and bramble, and the pet shop should be able to tell you what the foreign kinds eat – most will eat bramble. Put the twigs either in the damp peat or in a small jar of water, so they keep fresh. Even so, you should change them three or four times a week. If you don't keep the stems in water, spray the plants with a little water every day (an indoor plant spray or a squeezy bottle will be a fine applicator for this).

When your walking sticks are used to their home, they will probably walk about quite freely, but until then – and always when they are sleeping – they are extremely difficult to distinguish from their perch because of their super camouflage.

Some species of female stick insects (there are, in fact, very few males) will lay eggs that should hatch without the need of a male! This method of reproduction is called parthenogenesis. Stick insects reproduce very rapidly, and you may, in the end, have too many, in which case you can present some to your friends.

Some 'sticks' can also regrow a mutilated limb!

6

Rearing plant galls

Sometimes you will find strange-looking objects called galls, especially on oak trees. Some people think the galls are another form of the tree's fruit, but, of course, the only fruit borne by an oak tree is the acorn. One type of oak gall, usually known as an oak apple, is the result of a complicated interaction of the tree with the life cycle of an insect – and many other galls are also caused in some way by a plant and an insect.

In the case of the oak tree, a tiny insect called the gall wasp has bored a hole in an oak bud to lay its eggs. This upsets the tree and it makes the round object we call the oak apple. At first this is a fat, ball-shaped object, whitey-pink in colour. It grows in place of a bud. You will find oak apples when the young oak leaves are coming out, in late May. The oak apples usually grow quite low down, especially among hedgerows. Later on, by July, they have turned a yellowy-brown and are no longer shiny. You'll notice tiny holes in them, showing that the insects have flown.

It is fun to try and hatch out whatever has caused a gall. Obviously, you have to get them before the insect has flown – so the gall must have no telltale holes in it. Oak apples are best picked in June, marble galls at the end of August, and robin's pincushions, found on roses in July, mature in the winter and the insects emerge in the spring.

Robin's pincushion

Oak apples

Pick the gall and plant together, and put the whole thing in a jar of moist peat. Cover the plant and the top of the jar with butter muslin or cheesecloth, fixed on firmly with a rubber band around the neck of the jar. Moisten the peat frequently to keep the plant fresh.

If the galls have been knocked off their plant, you can rear them on damp blotting paper in a biggish jar, covered with a muslin lid.

Look at your galls every day until the occupant

emerges – who or whatever he is! Hatching time will vary; the average for an oak apple is six weeks, longer for a marble gall and a robin's pincushion takes a year to mature.

When the owner of the gall emerges, you should set him free. In fact, as well as the original owner, many other insects squat in galls to lay their eggs, cuckoo-fashion. So, what comes out may not in fact be the creature that caused the gall at all – which makes gall-rearing all the more fascinating!

Keep separate galls in separate homes, so you can decide who came from which gall!

7

Keeping insects in general

This chapter is about keeping insects generally, except for a few such as butterflies, ants, earwigs and so on which have chapters to themselves. Water insects are also dealt with separately in Chapter 14.

There are all sorts of insects you can have fun keeping for a little while, although it's not a good idea to try to keep adult dragonflies, mayflies, bees or wasps in captivity. If you know a beekeeper, he or she will probably be delighted to show you something of the workings of a hive. Occasionally, too, you may find the papery, football-like object that is a wasps' nest, and then you can watch the wasps' activity *very* cautiously from a distance. You can also encourage several types of non-hive bees to make their nests in a bee wall which you can make for them in your garden. There are also many insects that people often don't keep (such as plant bugs and beetles) because they don't look very attractive, but which are actually very interesting to watch. Remember, you can reassure an anxious family most insects are in fact very clean, and do not spread disease – with of course a few notable exceptions, such as flies.

An adult insect has three main parts to its body – a head, a middle part called the thorax, and a lower part called the abdomen. On its head it has long feelers called antennae, which it uses for smelling and feeling. Most adult insects have wings. And the trademark of all insects – six jointed legs – distinguishes them most clearly from other kinds of creepy crawlies, such as spiders, millipedes and woodlice.

Most insects are usually best kept only for short periods, so you can watch them grow, and then set them free. On the whole, they have brief lives although they may go through several stages before they become adult. Some, like butterflies, begin as an egg, which hatches into a larva (caterpillar). At the larva stage it eats a lot and moults several times as it grows. When it has finished growing it changes into a pupa (chrysalis); this is a resting stage in which the body of the larva breaks down and reforms to emerge as the adult winged insect. This change of shape is called a metamorphosis. Others, like the grasshopper and dragonfly, change from an egg to a nymph. A nymph is like its parents but it has no working wings. Its skin splits several times, and wings gradually appear. It grows larger and larger at each moult until it is an adult insect with fully developed wings, like its parents. A third type of insect, like springtails, and the silverfish sometimes found in larders, doesn't change at all at each moult, except to grow larger.

Most adult insects do not grow at all. Many (such as mayflies and non-biting midges) don't feed either. Some don't even have mouths. They don't need them because their main purpose in life is to find a mate and reproduce themselves before they die.

There are over 20,000 kinds of insects in Britain alone, while in the whole world there are around a million *known* species, let alone the countless *unknown* ones there are! In fact, throughout the world there are more kinds of insects than all the different kinds of reptiles, fish, birds and mammals put together. Remember insects can change colour and often shape as they grow into adults, and that often the male of a certain type of insect is a different colour from the female. A good book on identifying insects will be invaluable to you, especially in finding out what to feed them on. (There is a list of recommended books at the end of this book.)

If you decide to keep an insect or insects, you must give it surroundings as like its natural habitat as possible. Each kind of insect you decide to keep needs a *separate* insectarium, and you should transport them home in separate containers, too, because some insects are carnivores, and will eat each other. A good insectarium is any kind of glass or clear plastic container large enough for the insect to move around in. The picture shows some suggestions. You need transparent sides so that you can watch the insect easily – the insect isn't bothered about them! The chart on pages 52 and 53 gives a few pointers for keeping various types of common insect.If in doubt, consult the insect keeper at the zoo, or the Department of Entomology at a University or a natural history museum.

Usually, you should put peat or potting compost, which does not harden and become dusty even if it does dry out, on the bottom of the insectarium. Add some stones and plants, either sticking them in the damp peat or in a small jar of water plugged with a cardboard collar or cotton wool (sec page 13). You should always bring home some of the plants from the insect's home. Generally, keep the insectarium in a cool place, out of direct sunlight, but away from draughts, and keep it covered.

Give fresh food daily. Most insects eat only one kind

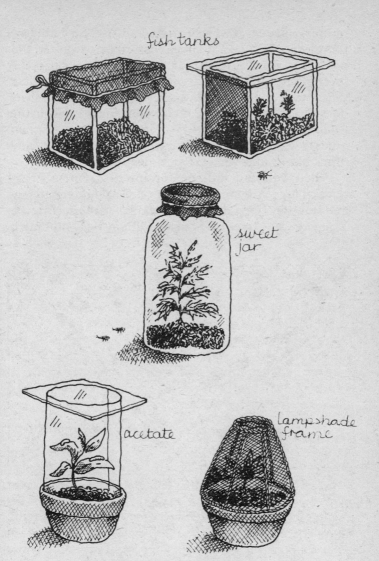

Various types of insectaria

47

of food. Many are herbivores, and will probably be found on their food plant. Others are carnivores and need dead insects, etc. If you are not sure which is the food plant, put in several plants from the place where you found the insect, and see which one it eats. If it doesn't eat any of them – and you can't discover the food plant from books – then let the creature go quickly where you found it. It will be unlikely to eat any other plant, and will starve to death in captivity.

When you are looking for insects, remember to replace logs and stones, and try not to damage plants and flowers. There are various ways of catching insects. You can beat trees and bushes with a stick, holding a

Insect beating tray

beating tray made from a large white sheet stretched over a wooden frame, or even a pale-coloured old umbrella upside down, under the branches. Various kinds of insect will tumble on to the sheet, and you can take home one or two of the ones that interest you. Remember to keep them in separate containers.

Page 19 explains how to set sugar and light-traps for moths. Your light-trap will certainly attract other insects as well. To catch crawling insects your best plan is to make a trap like the ones shown here. Place them near the bottom of a hedge, if you can.

Tin foil pie dish with hole in top

Insect traps

Generally, if you come across an insect you want to keep, the best method of catching it is the jam jar and postcard one. Hold the jar bottom upwards and pop it over the insect. An insect has a natural tendency to crawl upwards in the direction of any light there may be. So when it is in the top part of the jar, slide the postcard over the mouth of the jar and then carefully transfer the captive to the carrying jar.

With insects like ladybirds that stick close to the stem of a plant, you should take home the whole works – plant, insect and all! That way, you will also get the ladybird's food – the aphids feeding on the plant.

Carry your insects home in a box or screwtop jam jar. Line it with moss for their comfort, and handle the insects as little as possible. If you must handle them, use the paintbrush technique described on page 14. Once home, transfer them to your insectaria.

Remember always to make your insect pets as comfortable as possible. Give them the proper food and drink, and keep them clean. If you don't care for them well, they'll be restless and won't behave naturally. They may not even complete their life cycle.

Some bees, as we have said, don't live in hives but make or find holes in which to rear their young. You can encourage one such bee, the mason bee which has bright orange hairs, to nest where you want it to. Usually, a mason bee builds a cluster of cells out of mud and lays an egg in each. It stocks the cells with nectar and pollen. Sometimes it uses the space behind a doorpost or window frame where you can watch it coming and going. However, you may be able to persuade it to use an artificial hole. Tie together a cluster of plastic drinking straws. Position the bundle under a stone or among the roots of a tree, so that most of it lies in the dark, with one end open. (Alternatively, you could drill holes in a piece of wood.) With luck, the bee may find it and lay eggs in the tube. If this happens, after a bit you can pull out a tube and see what's happening inside. Make sure the bee is away at the time, though!

You can also try offering bumblebees an artificial nest, if you dig a small hole in the ground with a sloping entrance and put some torn-up bits of grass and moss outside for bedding. However, don't be too disappointed if your artificial nests aren't used. You can't force creatures to use them, but you can at least try. As you will find, being a naturalist takes enormous patience.

Some insects hibernate (spend the winter) in our homes. As well as butterflies sitting motionless in corners of your bedroom ceiling, you may find a lacewing or ladybird lurking in a crevice. Don't disturb them, but leave them there quietly until spring. Many will die, but the ones that don't will return to the garden and do lots of good – the butterflies helping to pollinate the flowers and lacewings and ladybirds gobbling up greenfly.

You can also encourage insects to visit your garden by planting some of the plants described on page 22.

Chart A

Creepy crawly	Type of cage	Peat, sand, etc.	Water	Food	Cage cover
BEETLES GENERALLY	Large glass cage (old fish tank or large coffee or sweet jar. A jam jar will do for small specimens). Twigs for climbing on	Cover sand with moss from damp wood	Keep sand moister than for grasshoppers	Moss, lettuce, etc.	Muslin cover
GROUND AND TIGER BEETLES	As beetles	As beetles, but peat on top of sand and dead leaves. Need warmth. Pieces of wood		Squashed flies, ants, etc.	None needed
LADYBIRDS (often found on rose shoots with aphids). Cut off whole shoot	Large cage, eg, old aquarium big enough for them to fly about	One or two branches to crawl on. Layer of peat	Moisten cage occasionally	Greenfly on rose shoots. Put shoot in jar of water with cardboard collar or tissue paper plug (see page 13). Note: when shoot is withered, keep it because possibly eggs have been laid	Muslin, etc, tied on firmly

52

	Container	Floor/substrate	Moisture	Food	Cover
STAG BEETLES	As beetles	As ground and tiger beetles		Adults will eat sugar. Grubs eat rotten wood	Firm cover with small holes
GRASSHOPPERS AND CRICKETS GENERALLY	As beetles	2.5 cm layer sand	Keep sand slightly moist	Fresh grass every day	Muslin or netting tied on firmly with string
BUSH CRICKETS (these are easy to catch, but are cannibals. Don't keep nymphs and adults together)	Large container (aquarium, etc). Twigs for climbing Don't keep in sun, but heat for short periods by putting near sunny window or desk lamp	Sand, covered with peat. Bits of corrugated cardboard	Sprinkle drops	Lettuce and occasional flies, grasshoppers, aphids, etc. Also occasional fruit, cheese, oatmeal	Strong terylene netting
FIELD CRICKETS	Small cage, eg largish jar	2.5 cm layer of grass	Keep cage slightly moist	Moist grass	None needed
HOUSE AND WOOD CRICKETS	Large glass cage	Sand or peat covered with dead leaves or crumpled paper	Keep moist. Put cage in warm, not hot, spot	Almost anything (especially cake and fruit). Not greasy food, as will mess up jar)	Wood crickets need none, but house crickets should be covered as they can fly
MOLE CRICKETS (can live 1–2 years)	Aquarium or large container	5 to 7 cm soil	Keep soil very moist, ie, muddy	Potatoes, or other root vegetables	Terylene netting – adults can fly

8

Keeping spinning spiders

'There came a big spider, and sat down beside her, and frightened Miss Muffet away.' Miss Muffet is not alone in her dislike of spiders. They must rank second only to snakes in being loathed by many, many people. There is something about a spider's long, wavy legs and scuttling movement that causes many an otherwise enthusiastic naturalist to cling to the nearest wall, shrieking for someone else to come and remove the beast! Of course, being good naturalists, they will only want the spider *removed*, not killed. In fact, spiders do virtually no harm and a great deal of good, as we shall see later on.

There is, of course, absolutely no basis for such fears – and people who do study spiders discover how truly fascinating they are.

Spiders are not, as often they are inaccurately thought to be, insects. Insects have six legs and are divided into three distinct parts – a head, thorax and abdomen. Unlike most adult insects, spiders have no wings. They belong to the class of creatures called Arachnids. They have eight legs, and only two body divisions, a head and thorax together, and a bulgy abdomen. Many insects pass through several distinct stages, changing their shape radically (from caterpillar to chrysalis to butterfly, for example). Spiders, like insects, start life as eggs but, unlike many insects, when they hatch they are perfect miniature spiders – and, although they shed their skin a number of times, they just grow gradually to be bigger and bigger spiders. In fact, the 'dead' spiders you may see around your shed or outbuildings may be dead, but are more likely to be the cast-off skins of spiders still very much alive, probably lurking somewhere looking at you.

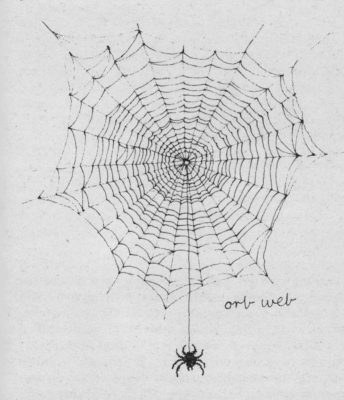

orb web

In Britain there are about 600 kinds of spiders, and, unlike some tropical species, all are harmless. In fact, they do a lot of good by eating insect pests. Moreover, unlike some insects, they never spread infection. They are very clean creatures. Unlike many insects, spiders are carnivores – they eat other creatures, never plants. The various types of web they build are for catching such prey.

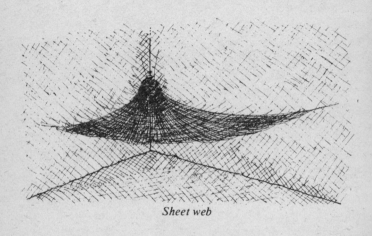

Sheet web

The big circular webs with many spokes you see glistening with dew on hedges and bushes, especially in late summer and autumn, are made by orb web spinners such as the Garden spider. This is also called the Cross spider because of the markings on its back. You can keep such spiders for a little while to study them, but it is much better and more rewarding to keep a sheet web spider. These are much more likely to spin you a fine web in captivity. They are not at all the same sort of spider as the hammock-web spiders which spin horizontal hammock-like webs in the garden. Nor, if you want a web built for you, is it worth trying to keep the spiders called Wolf spiders, which you often see streaking across the garden path. These hunting spiders do not build webs at all since they hunt their prey on foot.

The sheet web spiders are often called House spiders, although they are found not only in houses, but also in buildings around them, such as sheds and garages. These spiders are also called Cobweb spiders by spider experts. (Most people, of course, call all spiders' webs 'cobwebs'. Strictly speaking, they are right. The word 'cobweb' comes from the Old English word *cob*, meaning a spider – so 'cobwebs' originally just meant spider's web. However, spider-experts reserve the word 'cobweb' to describe the sheet webs spun by House spiders.)

You'll find the two kinds of sheet web spider which are most common, and easy to keep, in corners of sheds, in the garage, cellar or attic, or on any wall (inside or outside) which has nooks and crannies where the spider can spin its tube-shaped web. The silken tube gives the spider a place to lurk. From it spreads a sheet of silk, often triangular in shape because it has been spun at the corner of two walls.

Having found a spider, the next thing is to catch it! This can be quite difficult, although big spiders are easier to catch than nippy young ones. Whatever you do, don't try to pick a spider up, especially not by its legs. Spiders have a similar ability to lizards, in that they can shed a part of their body to avoid capture. They will drop a leg and, if they are still young, sub-sequently grow another. Sometimes, when moulting, a spider gets a leg jammed in its old skin and has to shed it in order to free itself.

Catching a spider

The best equipment for catching spiders is a clear plastic beaker or jam jar, and an old postcard – similar to the equipment you used for catching insects. The container needs to be clear so you can see what the spider is up to! Bring the postcard and container together on either side of the spider, even if you pinch some of the web in it. When the spider is in the container, put a lid on very smartly, as spiders put out 'safety lines'. These are almost invisible to you but spiders can zoom up and down them with amazing speed – and so out of your container! (Warning! One spider only at a time in a container or matchbox, or they may eat each other!)

Keep your spider in a 'spiderarium' – an old shoebox makes a fine basis for this. You will also need a kitchen paper or toilet tube, and some transparent plastic for the lid. Look at the pictures to see how to make your spiderarium. Leave the spiderarium in a quiet place like a garage or shed which is dark at night and where probably spiders already lurk naturally. Don't keep

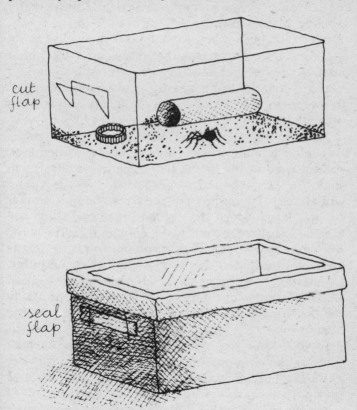

Spiderarium

shining lights on it, as this will disturb the spider. Soon the spider may find the tube and dive into it. After a bit, it should start to spin its web inside it, and then extend it to make a sheet web inside the main box.

When you see that the web has been started, you should give the spider some food – a live insect! Catch a fly with your beaker/postcard technique – a hoverfly settled on a flower is fairly easy. Have some water already in the beaker. Let the flower out carefully between the beaker and card. Shake the beaker about vigorously, keeping the card over the end. After about a dozen shakes, the fly will be wet and unable to fly, and you can tip it out and pick it up by one wing with a pair of tweezers. It will recover quite quickly and start to buzz and fly about.

Holding it gently in the tweezers, put it through the flap into the main spiderarium. If there is enough web spun yet, you can put the fly on the web itself. It will stick to the web and – hey presto! – the spider will attack! (If you just put the fly in the box, sooner or later it will touch the web and the same thing will happen.) If there are not really enough threads on the web to restrain the fly, it will probably buzz around the box, and the spider may have to chase it around a bit. Eventually, however, it will catch it and take it back to its den. Twenty-four hours or so later, you'll probably see the dried-up remains of the fly somewhere in the box.

If you don't like doing this to live flies, keeping spiders (like keeping snakes and lizards) is not for you, as they will usually only attack live prey – and *you* have to supply it.

An insect every other day should be enough for your spider. You can even go away and leave it for two or three weeks, so long as you top up its drinking bowl just before you go.

Gradually, your spider will build more and more web. Usually, it will work during darkness, sometimes improving the web by adding several tunnel entrances. The spider will scuttle away if you shine a light on it, but should appear eagerly when you put food on its web. Insert the food through the trapdoor. When the sheet web is good and solid, you can remove the lid of the box to insert the food. This will probably break some threads of the web attached to the lid, so at first the spider may not come out for a time. It will soon get used to the procedure and shoot out enthusiastically. Sometimes, if you have a female spider, you may be lucky and she will lay eggs.

When you have kept a few spiders in this way, you will soon discover how truly fascinating they are, and maybe you will be able to convert your spider-hating friends!

9

Making a snailery

Snails and slugs tend to be distinctly unpopular with gardeners, quite naturally when they find their young plants nibbled to bits by a snail's incredible 25,000 teeth! In fact, there are probably many more snails in a garden than even the most pessimistic gardener can imagine. One gardener who kept a count of the snails and slugs in his garden collected thousands and thousands a year! From which you can see that, if you want a pet that's easy to find – and slow enough to capture easily – a snail could be a good choice. Moreover, you will have removed a snail or two from your cabbage patch, which should make you popular with whoever does your garden. However, when snail-hunting, do remember most of them hibernate, so don't waste your time looking for them in winter.

Snails belong to a group of animals without backbones called molluscs. In fact, molluscs have no bones at all and build their own house to live in. Some other well-known molluscs are winkles, cockles and oysters. Snails usually live from two to five years, but can live much longer. They can move something up to 200 times their own weight! They move very slowly, dragging their houses with them, and leaving a shiny, slimy trail. The sticky fluid of the trail helps the snails to stick to things and move up, down and across just about *anything*. Remember that when you keep them!

There are a few other things to remember when keeping snails indoors. They can *eat* through just about anything, too. Edible snails used to be packed alive in wooden crates, but so many ate their way out of their containers that metal boxes had to be used instead. So it's useless to keep your snails in a cardboard box, or even a wooden one, just in case they munch their way out and slime up the furniture which will make you distinctly unpopular! You need a glass or plastic container, big enough for the snail to move about freely. An empty fishtank, or a big plastic or glass jar will do, but whatever you use *must* have a well-fitting, snail-proof lid, punched with small air holes.

Perforated zinc or wire netting with a small enough mesh (but not a gnawable fabric like muslin or cheese-cloth) will do if your container has no lid of its own.

Look for snails in dark, damp places – clinging to walls and stones, in the shade of trees and bushes, or in long, damp grass. If you're lucky, you'll see a silvery snail-trail. Follow it and you can track down the snail that made it. The best time to look for snails is in the evening or at night, or after rain. Collect the largest snails you can find, but not more than six. Carry them home in a large jar. (By the way, do make sure this travelling jar – and your permanent snailery – are rinsed *very* thoroughly before you put snails in them. Detergents and soap can be death to snails.)

As well as the snails, take home some of the plants, leaf mould and soil from where you found them, to make their snailery a home-from-home. These plants will probably be the ones on which they feed naturally. Early morning is a good time to see them feeding. You can also feed them on lettuce, parsley and rotting leaves, but an all-lettuce diet is not good for them, especially not for young snails who will probably not develop properly.

Most snails feed by night and rest by day. In the wild the same snail is often found on the same plant day after day. If you like, you can test this for yourself by marking a snail with a dab of paint (not near its opening, though) and seeing where it is each day.

Here are a few interesting facts.

Snails have the ability to mend small damage to their shells within two to three weeks, using a fluid produced by their bodies.

Most snails are hermaphrodites (they have both male and female organs in their bodies). However, they still need to mate with another snail, and each fertilizes the other's eggs. Young snails hatch, perfectly formed, with pink shells which are very small and soft.

Snails have been known to survive deep freezing for as long as $1\frac{1}{2}$ years – though this is not something you should try!

10

Making a wormery

The earthworm is a very common creepy crawly. We find earthworms when we turn over the soil; we see an unfortunate member of the family being yanked out of the ground by a determined blackbird; sometimes, after heavy rain, we find pale and swollen earthworms drowned or drowning in puddles – or even just lying on damp paving. This is a good opportunity to rescue those not quite dead and put them back on a piece of soft earth.

Earthworms come to the surface during rain probably because their burrows are full of water. Worms, like snails, are invertebrates, that is they have no backbones. They have no limbs, and move their bodies along by shortening and lengthening their segments. Like snails, they are hermaphrodites – each one being both male and female, and fertilizing the other's eggs.

Earthworms are sometimes called 'nature's ploughmen'. They turn over the soil and keep it alive and moving. They swallow it, pass it through their bodies and throw it out again as worm casts. While the soil is in their bodies, they digest any dead vegetable matter in it. This breaks down the minerals in soil needed by plants so that they can more easily be absorbed by the roots. Some gardeners don't much care for the look of their lawn with lots of worm casts on it, but the casts are in fact a very good sign. They prove that the earth is being shifted around, and kept fertile. Worms also drag down leaves and other plant materials which will fertilize the soil. There are probably several million earthworms in a hectare of soil – which is all to the good.

Wormery

If you keep three or four earthworms, you can watch this amazing earth-moving process. You'll need to make them a wormery. This can either be an upright construction of wood and glass, like the first ant palace (page 24), or a ready-made large glass or clear plastic container (such as a large sweet or coffee jar, or a plastic stacking biscuit container, old fish tank, etc). Fill the container with alternating layers of ordinary soil and lighter-coloured sand. Each layer should be about 2·5 cm thick, and sharply defined from the next layer. Finish the layers about 2·5 cm from the top. Then water them to make them damp, but not soggy.

To collect your worms, the best thing is to dig over a patch of soft, damp ground, and you will be bound to find some worms almost immediately. Put them on the top layer of your wormery, with some dead leaves and/ or grass cuttings. Fix a piece of muslin or cheesecloth over the top of the wormery with string or a rubber band. Cover it all up with a dark but not airtight cloth, or wrap brown wrapping paper round the wormery and fix it with sticky tape.

The next day you can take a peep and see how far the worms have got in jumbling the soil layers up. The worms are, in fact, eating the earth, and getting nourishment from the decaying matter in it. They will also come up to the top of the wormery to collect the leaves and clippings when they feel they need them. It is easier to watch this process if you keep your worms in a narrow wormery.

You'll have to keep the wormery mostly in the dark, but, like ants, worms don't seem to be too bothered by a red light. So when you want to watch them, use a red light bulb, or put red cellophane over a torch and hold it there with an elastic band.

All in all, a wormery is one of the easiest handy homes for creepy crawlies!

Worm fact – It isn't true that a worm cut in half will grow into two worms. However, if a short piece is accidentally cut off one end, the worm can grow a new 'head' or 'tail'.

11

Keeping grass snakes

Very occasionally, when walking in the country, you may come across a snake. You will then probably find you are one of two distinct categories of people! One type immediately shoots off in the opposite direction to the snake, shuddering in horror. Such a person you may call an ophiophobe (meaning a snake-fearer). The other type approaches the snake, fascinated but with caution, and discovers the beginnings of a love-affair with these scaly beasts. If you find you belong to the first category, don't bother with the first part of this chapter, although the second part from page 72 is useful if you want to keep other beasts in a vivarium. If, however, you find you like snakes, read on!

Snakes are reptiles. So are lizards, tortoises, turtles, and the lizard's cousin, the slowworm. Reptiles and amphibians (such as frogs, toads and newts) developed on earth many millions of years before birds and mammals. Some reptiles such as tortoises are still much the same in shape and looks as they were then. On the whole, today's reptiles come from warm countries. They have dry, scaly skins, whereas amphibians have moist, soft ones. Both are cold-blooded creatures – their body temperature does not stay the same all the time as yours – or your cat's or dog's – does. A reptile's temperature varies according to the temperature of its surroundings. When the weather is cold, the creature is cold and therefore sluggish. When the weather is hot its temperature rises and it is active. So reptiles tend to bask in the sun to warm up, but when the weather gets too hot for them they find a patch of shade to lie in to cool off. It's important to remember this fact when keeping any reptile.

There are only three native kinds of snake in Britain (Ireland has none). One kind, the adder (also called the viper) is poisonous. You should not try to keep one in captivity, pick it up or go near it at all (and this goes for all poisonous snakes, many of which are imported). You should recognize the adder fairly easily by the V or X on its head, and by the dark zigzag pattern along its back.

There is also a rare snake, the smooth snake, which is not poisonous but if picked up may discharge a nasty-smelling liquid. It is found only in Southern England and, because it is so rare, it is now protected by law and you must not collect it. Its colour varies from grey to reddy-brown. As it has dark spots along the back and a dark patch on each side of, and on top of, the head, it is sometimes mistaken for the adder. It's as well therefore to play safe and steer clear of all such snakes just in case!

The other common British snake is the grass snake. It varies in colour but the upper side is usually olive brown with vertical black bands along each side. It has two yellow or orange crescent-shaped patches on the nape of its neck, with black triangles behind. It is not poisonous, but, if in doubt whether it's an adder, play safe! Grass snakes can, in fact, be very good pets to keep, even for a beginner. The only real problem you may have to overcome is opposition from snake-hating members of your household! Grass snakes are rather shy at first, but after they get used to you they become very placid and long-suffering. They may even wrap themselves affectionately round your arms and neck. (Ophiophobes: if you forced yourself to read this far you are allowed to shudder here!)

Your grass snake will live best in a vivarium (a special home for creatures needing more than an ordinary box or cage). Do make sure your vivarium is secure against escape, though, as nothing puts even the most tolerant family off more than your slithery pet peering at them from a quiet corner of the living room. The well known naturalist Gerald Durrell tells how when he was a boy he dumped some water snakes in the family bath as a temporary home, forgot to tell anyone and badly upset the first member of his family who wanted a bath.

Sometimes you may find a worm-like creature you think is a snake, but which is the legless lizard called a slowworm (see Chapter 12). In fact, the slowworm is not only not a snake, it's neither slow, nor a worm, either!

A vivarium can be constructed in various ways, and with modifications used for a variety of pets including lizards, frogs and toads. People often use an old aquarium (without the water, of course), fit it with a lid and heater, and think that they have a satisfactory vivarium. However, although this may do for some species, an all-glass vivarium is not at all perfect. There is a terrific heat loss through the glass, and this also applies to another popular vivarium, the all-metal cage (which can also overheat!). There can be great amounts of condensation too, which will cause a health hazard to snakes and lizards which like perfectly dry conditions.

If you do have an old metal-framed aquarium avail-

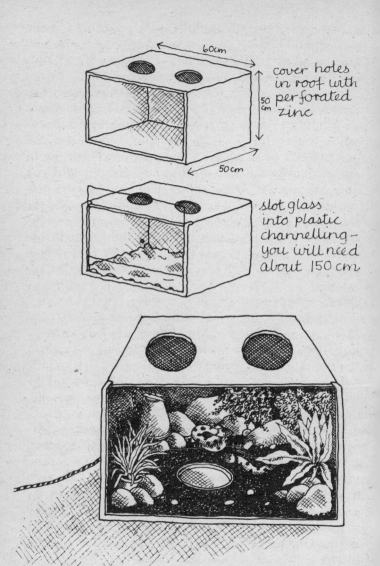

60cm

cover holes
in roof with
perforated
zinc

50 cm

50 cm

slot glass
into plastic
channelling –
you will need
about 150 cm

How to make a vivarium

able, however, you could with help probably remove two or three of the glass sides and replace with two sides of wood and one of perforated zinc. You'll also need to add a close-fitting lid.

Generally, what sort of vivarium you make depends a lot on what materials you have available, how handy you are, and how much help you can enlist from 'do-it-yourself' grown-ups or older brothers and sisters. You can construct a wooden vivarium from scratch, about 60 cm long by 50 cm wide and 50 cm deep. Or if you already possess a strong crack-free wooden box (not plywood, though, which warps) you could replace the front with a piece of glass, and make two holes in the top and cover these with perforated zinc. Don't use wire netting, as many reptiles, especially snakes, will rub against it and damage their snouts. Also, if the mesh is too large, some snakes may ooze their way through it.

Another super ready-made base for a vivarium is an old-fashioned glass-fronted kitchen cupboard – or indeed any kitchen cupboard if you can replace the door with a glass panel.

Paint the inside of the vivarium, especially the wooden parts, with several coats of gloss paint (poly-urethane paint is fine). White, although often used, is not really ideal, partly because it gets dirty and partly because it reflects so much light that the inhabitants tend to hide away.

For many creatures that live in a vivarium, you'll have to fix a heater of some sort. (Fortunately, your grass snake won't need heat.) The illustration on the next page shows one way of making a heater, but other suggestions are a heating cable covered with lead or plastic coating which can be bent gently and covered with a layer of sand, or a small heating plate as used by

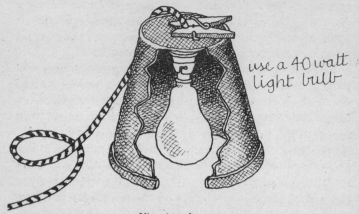

use a 40 watt light bulb

Vivarium heater

amateur winemakers is excellent. Switch the heating off at night. A light over the top will add to the warmth, and also help show the inhabitants off better. *Always* get a grown-up who really knows about electricity to fix the heater and lighting for you, and do remember that electricity can be *very* dangerous.

Now to furnish your vivarium. The chart on page 92 gives some hints. For creatures such as snakes and lizards that need dry conditions, you should cover the floor with fish tank gravel (not sand). You'll need to sift it first to remove any impurities. Every so often, replace it with fresh gravel. Or wash and dry it – leave it for a week until perfectly dry before putting it back. This means you'll need at least two lots of gravel. Creatures such as frogs that like damp conditions need an extra layer of dampish peat over the gravel. Squeeze out most of the moisture before you put the peat in.

Plants are generally for decoration – and you can even use plastic ones – the inhabitants won't mind! For an unheated terrarium, grasses, heather, ivy and dwarf juniper are good, while sansivieria (mother-in-law's tongue), philodendron, and tradescantia will do in both heated and unheated spots. Keep them in pots so you can change them easily and frequently.

Put in some rocks (one or two especially near the heater for basking) and include some tunnel-shaped ones, so shy creatures can shelter under them. Don't use cement (man-made) rocks, nor any with lots of lime in them. You can also use cut bark (from florists' shops) either on the ground as shelter tunnels, or stuck to the wall of the vivarium to help creatures such as snakes in sloughing. This shedding of the skin occurs every few weeks, and the creature does need a rubbing post to help peel it off. A rough-barked chunk of tree will help as well. Some reptiles, including your grass snake, will appreciate a branch of tree wedged across the vivarium to climb on and around. Don't put it too near the heater, though, or you'll have sizzled snake!

Grass snakes really enjoy hiding and climbing. They also adore a dip, so give them a pool big enough to swim around (which they do very elegantly). Some-times a grass snake stays underwater for half an hour or so. After its dip, it will enjoy sunbathing in a patch of real or artificial sun (from an infra-red lamp or bulb). In the wild you will often find grass snakes near ponds or marshy places. For the vivarium 'pond', a shallow plastic box or plastic cat litter tray sunk in the gravel and kept full, so the snake can submerge, will do fine. Put the 'pond' halfway between the vivarium side and the heater. You'll have to change the water frequently, as your slithery friend will most probably use it as a lavatory!

Daily fresh water is essential for most vivarium animals. Also, unless perfectly dry conditions are necessary, it's a good idea to spray the vivarium plants to keep a moist atmosphere. As for food, grass snakes may eat only once a week. In the wild their food would be living things – such as live frogs, fish, newts (though not the Great Crested variety which exudes a nasty substance). You'll need a regular supply of live food and, unless you are able to train your snake to take pieces of meat and fish waved about on the end of a stick, you have a tricky dilemma. Either you put the frogs, fish, etc, into the vivarium alive, and let the snake eat them when it wants – which can be upsetting to watch, or (which may be even more upsetting) you have to kill the prey painlessly yourself, and serve it up still fresh so it has the right scent and body heat. Think this out very carefully *before* you get your snake. If you don't think you can face either alternative, then snake-keeping is not for you.

If you decide to leave the prey alive, remember to give *it* some food, too, to make its last hours (or even days, if the snake isn't very hungry) as pleasant as possible.

With luck your grass snake should live happily and healthily for a number of years. A healthy grass snake has clean skin, bright eyes and sticks its tongue out often. If at any time yours looks odd, it may be sick. Then, as with any domestic pet, but especially with reptiles, you should consult your vet immediately. If he is not a snake-expert himself, he will know who to ask, perhaps the reptile keeper at a zoo.

12

Lizards and slowworms

Sometimes, on a warm, sunny afternoon, especially on heathland, you may almost step on a lizard basking in the sun. As soon as it spots you, it will scuttle away, however. Lizards are very difficult to catch but, if you are lucky enough to do so, or get one by chance, you could keep it for a while in a vivarium.

Remember you should never grab a lizard by its tail, however tempting it may look. Lizards have the ability to shed their tails to escape capture. A new tail will eventually grow but, in the meantime, you will have lost your lizard. (By the way, no other part of the lizard's body will grow again – if it loses a leg or toe, that's that!)

Lizards are reptiles like snakes. They need to warm up and cool off their body temperatures according to the weather. Lizards found in Britain are the Common Lizard and the Sand Lizard. The Common Lizard is about 15 cm long and, and lives in rough grassland and moorlands, and the outskirts of woodland. Its favourite food is insects, including moths, and spiders. It also eats larvae and earthworms which it swallows whole. In captivity it needs a drinking bowl – a soup plate or glass pie-dish will do fine. Never use an enamel pie-dish as this may chip and foul the water.

The Sand Lizard is a little larger than the Common Lizard. You can recognize it by the 'eye-spots' on its underside (these are dark rings with white centres). During the summer the male turns a bright green on its underneath and sides. The Sand Lizard lays eggs, unlike the Common Lizard which produces live young. It lives on sand-dunes and heaths, in England only, and is now very rare. It is protected by law and, if you should ever be lucky enough to find one, you must not collect it.

The Wall Lizard and the Green Lizard which live naturally on the continent of Europe are sometimes sold in Britain in pet shops.

On the whole, all lizards prefer their prey to be live – or, at any rate moving, which means, if the prey is dead, it has to be moved about by you on the end of a pair of tweezers. So, keeping lizards is not to everyone's taste! Try feeding yours live grasshoppers, flies, spiders, woodlice, worms and small moths. Don't feed butter-flies because, although the lizard likes them, they are getting very scarce these days and should be protected.

Make sure all the food is a reasonable size for the lizard. If it's too big, it frightens the lizard and is not usually eaten. Put live food in a dish with sides unclimb-able by larvae, but not unclimbable by the lizard which must *see* its food to want to eat it.

In general, lizards need a vivarium that is warm and dry, and heated (see page 73). Most don't require a swimming pool, just a bowl of clean, fresh drinking water. Line the bottom of the vivarium with fine gravel. Give the lizard some rocks (not made of cement, how-ever, nor stones with a lot of lime in them) so it can shelter under them. Plant the vivarium with suitable plants in pots, if you like, such as houseleeks, London pride, stonecrops, etc. Add clumps of grass to copy the lizard's natural surroundings. Like frogs, lizards will hibernate under cold conditions but, if they are kept warm indoors in a heated vivarium, they will remain active.

Slowworms are cousins of the lizards, and are sometimes also called blindworms. They are neither slow, blind nor a worm! They are, in fact, legless lizards. Like all lizards, they have movable eyelids, so you can easily distinguish them from snakes. Despite their 'blindworm' nickname, they have large, good eyes. They're not slow, either. The word slowworm actually comes from an Anglo-Saxon word *sléan* meaning to strike. Apparently, the Anglo-Saxons thought the creatures were poisonous, which, of course, they are not. They are quite harmless, but rather clumsy.

Slowworms are often found at twilight in damp, shady spots – deciduous woodland, gardens, hedgerows and also on woodland paths where they often bask. They also hide under flat stones and discarded pieces of corrugated iron where they lie to absorb warmth. Colours vary from silvery fawn to a coppery tint; sometimes the females have a dark stripe along the back. Usually, a slowworm is just over 30 cm long. It has smooth, shiny scales unlike snakes which are matt. To catch it, grasp it just behind the head. If it coils around your hands, never try to straighten it out. Handle it carefully. If you don't it may break off its tail part – like the lizard it is.

A slowworm likes a shady vivarium, though it will bask from time to time. Give it an open-topped vivarium, or a damp, unheated container, with lots of pot plants. It will eat slugs, small snails, and insects, and will learn to take mealworms and earthworms. Don't keep it in the same cage as smaller lizards, as it may snap them up, thinking they are worms.

Slowworms usually settle down well in captivity, and live a long time. One even lived for 54 years! If you have a pair, they may even breed. Like the Common Lizard, they have their young alive. It's safest to separate the babies from their parents, and feed them on young slugs, chopped worms and small insects.

In summer, if your garden is walled in, you could let your slowworm have the run of it where it will be a very useful and popular pet, eating all sorts of garden pests. You may have to explain to visitors that it is not a snake, though!

While on the subjects of reptiles, may I put in a plea for some foreign ones – tortoises and terrapins which are frequently captured and imported as pets. Many thousands die through unsuitable feeding and care. It is believed that eighty per cent do not survive their first winter. In fact, the Royal Society for the Prevention of Cruelty to Animals doesn't encourage this trade at all. However, if you find, or have given to you, or absolutely cannot resist buying a tortoise or terrapin, *do* read up some of the books on the subject before you take on the responsibility of caring for it. Or send off for the RSPCA's information booklet which is excellent.

13

Keeping frogs, toads and newts

Tadpoles are one of the most commonly kept wild pets, taken very much for granted – and yet I personally am constantly enthralled by their everyday but truly miraculous change from swimming, legless, gill-breathing tadpoles to land-based, legged, air-breathing froglets.

Frogs, toads and newts are all amphibians – they start life as tadpoles swimming in water and breathing like fish through gills behind the head. They then grow legs, hop on to land and breathe air as we do. When adult they live most of the time on land in damp places and return to the water only to breed. They lay eggs called spawn, but in different ways. Frog spawn is laid in very shallow ponds as large jelly-like clusters (rather like the tapioca pudding of school dinners which is nicknamed after it!). Sometimes frog spawn is rather grubby and not easy to see. There will be about 4,000 eggs in a cluster of spawn.

Toad spawn – which is poisonous to most creatures that might eat it – comes in long strings of jelly up to 4 metres long, wound round pond weeds. It is usually laid in deeper ponds or running water. Newt eggs are laid single on the leaves of pond plants which the female newt folds over to protect them.

Although I have to confess that I once *bought* some frog spawn for a few pence from the pet department of a large London department store, and reared sixty-seven froglets from it, the more traditional way of getting spawn is to collect it from a pond with a net (see page 99 for how to make a net).

The best time to look for frog spawn is March and April. Toad spawn comes a little later, up until the end of May. Put the spawn in a jam jar with some of the pond water. You should also take along a bucket to collect some extra water for your tadpoles' home. Do be *very* careful not to fall in. If you have to wade into the pond (which really shouldn't be necessary, especially when collecting frog spawn) test the depth with a long pole first. Don't use logs or stones as stepping stones without trying them first.

Take only a little spawn, and return any surplus to the pond quickly so you don't denude that area of tadpoles. Frogs are getting less common than they used to be, partly because there is so much polluted water about.

If the spawn in the pond has already hatched, you could collect a few tadpoles in your net, put them *quickly* into the jam jar of water, and take them home to rear. (You can tell the difference between frog and toad tadpoles if you look at their tails. The toad tadpole has a tail with a rounded tip. The frog tadpole's is more pointed.)

Back at home, if you have a magnifying glass you can look at the spawn and work out about how long ago it was laid – and so how long it will be before it hatches.

If the egg is half white and half black, it has only just been laid.

If it is black all over, and round, it is two or three days since it was laid.

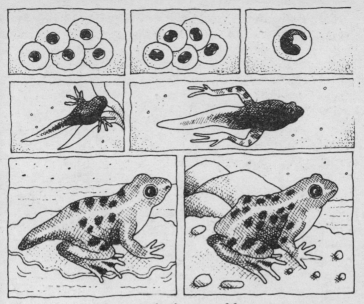

Stages in development of frog

If it is black, but dumb-bell-shaped – it has been laid about a week.

If it has a head and tail – it is about ten to twelve days old. Eggs should hatch about fourteen days after being laid. The picture shows their stages of growth.

Keep your spawn in an old aquarium – or a large plastic box. Don't use a goldfish bowl for tadpoles (nor indeed for any water creature, even – and especially not – for goldfish) as its shape doesn't allow enough oxygen to get into the water. If possible, use water from a pond, and fill the container to about 10 to 15 cm deep. If you do have to use tap water, let it stand for a few days before putting the tadpoles in it. If the water is very chlorinated, boil it first, taking care not to scald yourself. (Of course, you shouldn't really collect tadpoles

83

before the water is ready, but spawn is all right if you keep it in the pond water in the jam jar.)

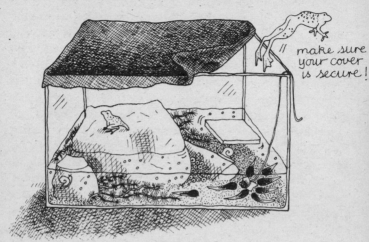

make sure your cover is secure!

Home for tadpoles, frogs or newts

Finish off your tadpoles' home as shown in the picture. Remember you *must* give them a stone or stones with sides that slope gently and are preferably not too smooth, or a floating piece of wood. The froglets will need these to clamber out onto when they grow their legs and start breathing air. Otherwise they'll drown, and you'll find sad little bloated corpses floating on top of the water – and I'm afraid it will be your fault!

In a warm room, your tadpoles may actually hatch as soon as a week or ten days after being laid. It's best not to try to rear them all. Keep six or eight, and take the rest back to the pond where you got them. I must confess I didn't know this when I reared my sixty-seven, but then I did separate the hatchlings into several cake tins (luckily, we don't eat much cake!) and, as I remember, I did lose a few.

When they first hatch, the tadpoles will eat the pond plants you've put in the aquarium. In an emergency I have known them eat lettuce, but, as with all creatures, food from their natural habitat is a hundred times better than artificial, that is substitute, food. After about a week, and certainly when their legs start to appear, they'll need raw meat as well. Tie a small piece of raw meat on to a thread and dangle it in the water. You could also use a live earthworm, but this is rather unkind to the earthworm, and not necessary as it is with creatures that take only live food. A recently dead earthworm – perhaps washed out by the rain – would be acceptable, though make sure it isn't one that's been poisoned by garden wormkiller. Waterfleas are good, too. You can buy these from aquarium shops – they are called daphnia. Feed them live to the tadpoles, who will gobble them up whole most enthusiastically. If you don't give them meat at this stage, your tadpoles will turn cannibal and eat each other (which they will do in any case if one dies!).

Replace the dangling meat every day, before it goes bad, or your tadpoles will die from foul water. Top the water up with new from time to time. If it's tap water, make sure it's been treated (see page 83). You must also change the water if it goes foul.

As soon as the tadpoles grow legs – and sooner if your cat is likely to use them for angling practice – put a cover on the tank. This should be a piece of glass or plastic, resting on small bits of wood to allow some air in. You could use perforated zinc or butter muslin. If you don't have a cover, you'll probably have the modern version of one of the plagues of Egypt – tiny froglets hopping all over your kitchen floor, that is if they haven't killed themselves in their harakiri leap for freedom. At that leg-growing stage, too, it's *essential* they have something easy to climb onto to get out of the water, so they don't drown. Indeed, it's said that the easier it is for them to get ashore, the quicker will be their change from tadpole to frog – average time three months.

Sometimes tadpole development can be very erratic and worrying. When I was a child, I had a batch of tadpoles that grew one back leg only, staying that way for days (even weeks, if I remember right). It was probably some deficiency in their diet, but eventually, in desperation, I took them back to the pond and hoped for the best. Goodness knows whether I had inadvertently crippled them for what was left of their short lives – three-legged froglets no doubt becoming easy prey for predators. Hopefully, this won't happen to yours.

When they have all four legs and are perfect miniature replicas of their parents, the best thing is to take them back to the pond where you got them, and let them go. Although you can keep fully grown frogs in a vivarium (see page 72), these tiny froglets, only about a centimetre long, need tiny live insects and small earthworms to eat. They are really quite difficult to feed and will probably die if you keep them any longer. So, put them down by the side of the pond in long, damp grass and steel yourself to watch them hop away.

Of course, if you have a pond in your garden, you have a ready-made place to let them go, but if you have reared a lot, you should still take some back to their original pond, so as not to unbalance its ecology.

Toad tadpoles are similar in their requirements, but

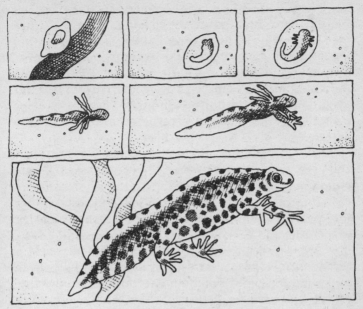

Stages in development of newt

are much larger, more bulbous chaps. Newt tadpoles hatch between one and three weeks after the eggs are laid. The tadpoles are thin, transparent creatures. From the start they eat tiny creatures from the water-weeds and then graduate to water fleas and tiny worms. Their two *front* legs grow first, and then lungs and back legs develop. Then, as with frogs, the gills disappear, and the young newt is ready to leave the water by July or August. However, some late developers stay in the water until the following year.

Adult newts spend spring and early summer in the water to spawn. Then they lose their bright spring colours and leave the water to spend the rest of the year on land in shady places. If you want to keep adult newts for a while, the best time to catch them is from March to June while they are still in the water. You can either use a net, or a worm on a bit of cotton, with a matchstick float. Pull the line ashore before the newt has time to spit it out again. Be very careful not to hurt the newt's mouth if you have to free it from the bait, although often it will disgorge itself. Take the newt or newts home in a plastic box full of water weed and take some extra pond water in a bucket.

There are three kinds of British newt – the Great Crested (the largest), Smooth, and the Palmate (smallest). Male newts develop splendid crests along their backs and tails during the breeding season, but lose them in late summer when they leave the water. Do not collect the Crested newt, which is becoming rare. The Smooth newt is still quite common.

The picture on page 84 shows you how to set up an aquarium to keep your adult newts during their 'watery' phase. The newtery does need to be in an aquarium or similar container as newts need a fair amount of space – about 60 cm long by 30 cm wide by 20 cm deep is about right for two or three adult newts. It will need a cover, either net or perforated zinc or a large piece of card with air holes, to stop them climbing out, or at any rate to stop your nosey moggy fishing them out. Put in a 2·5 cm layer of sand and gravel, together with several pots of rooted aquarium or pond plants. The water should be only about 10 to 12 cm deep, with an island at one end. This should be about 25 or 30 cms across, made of gravel and largish pebbles and stones and held in place with a piece of turf. An old log would also make a good island – both the turf and the log would have food in them. Let the edges of the island slope, so the newts can clamber out easily. An alternative is a floating raft of wood or polystyrene. You absolutely must give newts the opportunity of climbing out of the water or they may drown. Give them also a shelter or two on the island made with flat stones.

Keep the newtery in a light place, but not in direct sunlight or in a hot place. Feed them on earthworms, water fleas, mosquito larvae and small bits of raw meat. Replace the bits of meat frequently, so they don't foul the water. When your newts start spending the whole time on their island, they are telling you they can't stand their watery life any longer and may drown if you leave them in it. It's best then to take them back to where you found them, so they can prepare to hibernate. As they are largely nocturnal, ideally you should release them in the evening.

If at this stage you feel you *must* keep them longer, transfer them to a fairly damp vivarium (see page 74). You could use your drained aquarium for this, if you have nothing else suitable. Cover the bottom with earth and put in moss, bark and stones. Leave a bowl of water in one corner and change it frequently. While on land, the newts will also eat small caterpillars, worms, centipedes and other creatures. Fortunately, they will also learn to take mealworms (see Chapter 19).

Spray the vivarium every day with water to keep it damp. You should be able to keep the newts until spring when they'll want to go back to the water. As winter approaches place the vivarium in a cold (frost proof) place such as a garage or a garden shed, so your newts can hibernate.

Grown frogs and toads (that is, ones caught fully adult, not ones reared from tadpoles) can also be kept in a vivarium, but in dampish conditions. Be sure if you have several frogs that they are roughly similar in size, or the larger ones might eat the smaller. (This also applies when keeping lizards.) Feed the frogs on insects and worms, slugs and snails.

They will go into hibernation in October so, as with newts, adult frogs and toads should be placed in a cold garage or shed for the winter.

Frogs and toads can also be kept as 'liberty pets' near a pond in the garden, or (especially toads) in your greenhouse or conservatory where they'll act as unpaid but enthusiastic slug-eaters. You have to warn people they are there, though, or they may tread on them.

In the garden, if you want to keep them to study for a while, you can make them an enclosed run of stones or wood with unclimable, and unjumpable, walls about 1 metre or so high. Give them damp and shady conditions and a moist, cool home as you would in a vivarium. Hot sun will kill them unless they can retreat into the shade. Spray their home with a fine mist of water every day. (Incidentally, an amphibian breathes through its skin, so try not to handle it more than necessary, and always use damp hands.)

The frogs will need some swimming water, large and deep enough for them to immerse, to keep their skins always damp. They need much more damp than toads. A simple 'pond' made of a large piece of polythene sheeting lining a hole in the ground and weighed down with stones will do fine. Put a few stones and rocks in the middle for islands.

Unless your pets are free-range, you'll have to catch their food yourself. You can also train them to eat mealworms and maggots (see Chapter 19).

To find a toad, your best plan is to visit ponds in the breeding season (end March until May) at night. (Be *especially* careful not to fall in.) By day, toads hide in holes in the ground, but at night you may hear a male croaking. Shine a torch at him. He won't move while the light is shining in his eyes, and you can pick him up.

Take him home in a wet plastic box (eg, a sandwich box) with air holes punched in the lid. Remember, however, that the Natterjack toad is now protected by law in Britain, and may not be collected. You can recognize the Natterjack by the yellow line running down its back. It is found mainly in sandy, coastal areas in Britain.

There are a lot of silly stories about toads being poisonous, giving you warts, and so on. These are not true and you can tell other people this. However, although the secretions from a toad's skin are not poisonous, don't let them get in your eyes. In fact, they give out so unpleasant a taste that a dog which picks up a toad will never do it again!

Chart B Vivarium creatures

Animal	Special conditions	Peat, gravel, etc	Plants	Food
FROGS AND TOADS (ADULT)	Frogs need small pond with an island for sitting on. Toads need bowl for drinking water. Keep in shade.	Gravel with layer of damp peat over. Frogs need damper conditions than toads.	Pond weeds. Shade plants with big leaves, eg, cheese plant.	Insects, worms and mealworms, Tubifex (in water), raw meat, gnat larvae. Feed once or twice a week.
NEWTS	An aquarium or large bowl with an island during breeding season. Transfer to vivarium when they crawl out of water	2·5 cm layer of sand and gravel	Rooted aquarium or pond plants	Tubifex, gnat larvae (in water); raw meat, raw fish, or small live fish (guppies, etc). When on land, worms
LIZARDS	Rocks, sticks and branches. Put in warm place for a few hours each day. Water dish	Dry soil. Fine gravel	Philodendron and ivy. Dry stuff, eg, bracken or heather for sloughing	*Live* insects, very fond of spiders. Worms for large lizards, snails and slugs. Feed about twice a week
SLOWWORMS	As lizards	Layer of peat	See grass snake	Slugs are favourite, worms
GRASS SNAKES	As lizards, but include pool	Gravel	Small plants in pots for shade	Live fish (guppies, etc)

14

Keeping pond creatures

Apart from tadpoles and freshwater fish (see Chapter 15), there are many other fascinating water creatures you can keep and watch – either in a pond in the garden or in an indoor aquarium. Water skaters, water boatmen, water snails, great diving beetles, caddis fly larvae – all are interesting to keep, although you must be careful not to mix them up, or they may eat each other. The great diving beetle and the dragonfly nymph in particular are ferocious predators.

You can make a small outdoor pool quite easily by digging a hole in the ground and lining it first with sand or old newspapers. Then line it with a sheet of strong polythene. Be careful not to tear the polythene nor to leave pointed stones underneath it which might puncture it. Cover the edges of the polythene with stones and rocks, partly to weigh it down and partly to make it look more natural. Set a few pond plants in small flowerpots and sink them to the bottom. You can also leave a few water plants floating as cover for the inhabitants. If possible, fill with pond water, or water from a rain butt. If you have to use tap water, let it stand for a few days and, if highly chlorinated, boil it first. The pond level should be kept up fairly well by rainfall but, if there is no rain for a time, top up so it doesn't get stagnant.

Insects such as gnats and midges will soon find their way there and dance above it in a cloud. After a while they will probably lay their eggs in the pool. When they hatch, you will see tiny larvae wriggling about or hanging from the surface. After another three weeks or so, they will turn into pupae, and eventually flying adults will emerge. Because they fly, you must keep them out of doors, but if you can't make an actual pond, a large jar will do just as well. For this you will probably have to collect eggs from a pond, as the insects are less likely to lay in the jar. Sometimes you can find them in a rainwater butt.

You can also keep in your outdoor pool some of the creatures mentioned for keeping in an aquarium.

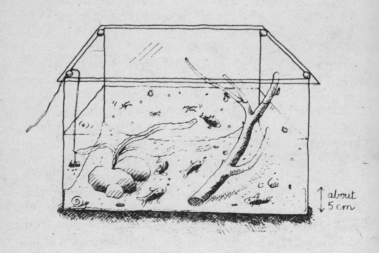

Home for pond creatures or freshwater fish

Set up an aquarium for pond creatures as in the picture, and follow the same principles given in more detail in Chapter 15. You need about 5 cm of washed sand or gravel, stones, water plants for oxygenating the water and providing some of the food, and so on. Again, if you have to use tap water, treat it as described on page 93. Always try to include some water snails, often found in ponds lurking under lilypads or mixed up with water weed. You can scoop these up in an old kitchen sieve. Snails are not only interesting in themselves but, even more important, they will help keep your tank clean. However, they do need a fair amount of space.

Visit a pond with a very fine-meshed fishing net (made of butter muslin or cheesecloth) and catch some creatures that interest you. Keep diffcrent creatures in separate containers, in case they gobble each other up. If they are ones that can, or will later, fly, put a cover on the tank, but do remember it must let air through.

With some very tiny creatures, you don't need to use a tank. A plastic box (with lid pierced for airholes) or even a plastic margarine pot will do well.

On page 96 is a chart showing the sort of food each kind of creature will eat. Very tiny ones and fry may need some 'infusoria soup' (see page 120).

Unless you keep the creatures only a few days, you'll have to clean the tank out occasionally, first transferring the creatures to another container. As usual, treat any tap water, and if you use any soap or detergent when cleaning, rinse it out very thoroughly.

Chart C Pond Creatures

Creature	Container	Peat, gravel, etc	Plant	Water level	Food	Cover
CADDIS FLY LARVAE (will do better in running water)	Small fish tank or large plastic container	Sand, plus small stones, shells, bits of wood, plastic, beads, etc, for making their protective cases	Water plants	10 to 15 cm	Water weed	No cover
DRAGONFLY NYMPH (carnivorous)	Small tank or large jam jar. Put in upright stick for creature when it has shed its skin	Sand	Water plants	About 15 cm	Maggots, tadpoles, small fish	Muslin or perforated zinc
GREAT DIVING BEETLE (very fierce! Keep by itself) and WATER BOATMAN	Small tank	Sand all over, plus a bank of it piled up at one end	Water weed held down with stones	15 to 22 cm	Maggots or raw meat attached to cotton and changed daily	Perforated zinc (can fly)

15

Keeping freshwater fish

Many people keep goldfish and other imported cold-water fish. Others enjoy keeping tropical fish with their bright colours and varying shapes, but these need special and expensive equipment – heaters, thermostats, aerators, and so on. But there are several native freshwater fish anyone can keep fairly cheaply and easily – fish such as sticklebacks (tiddlers), minnows, bleak, and young gudgeon. With a little patience – and a net! – you can catch these from ponds and streams.

As when keeping any other pet, it's important to have your fish's home ready *before* you get it. This is especially important with freshwater creatures, so they have to endure as little time as possible in their travelling container. So find as large a fish tank or plastic wide-topped container as you can. It should not be a goldfish bowl. This should *never* be used for any fish or other water creature, as its narrow neck doesn't give them enough surface air. Whether you get a proper fish tank (called an aquarium) or improvise one, it should, if possible, be plastic. It will then be lighter to move and less likely to break or spring a leak.

Wash the tank out thoroughly, and rinse away absolutely all traces of any detergent or soap, as these are very harmful to all freshwater or marine creatures.

Put in a 2·5 cm layer of clean, well washed aquarium sand (not sea sand) or gravel. You can get these from an aquarium shop. Add a few well-scrubbed rocks and stones, but don't use man-made lumps of concrete or any stone containing a lot of lime. These may release harmful substances into the water and harm the fish.

If you can, get pond water (a few bucketsful), and at the same time collect some pond plants. These will act partly as food for the fish, and partly (and more importantly) to aerate the water. If you can't get pond water and have to make do with water from the tap, boil it to get rid of any chlorination (don't burn or scald yourself, though). Then let the water stand for a few days. Of course, rainwater from a water butt would be a good substitute for pond water. Do make sure, both when you get your pond water and plants, and later when you catch your fish, that you don't fall into the pond! Test the depth of the water with a long pole before wading in, and don't stand on any logs or stones without making absolutely sure they are firm and won't tip you in.

The best way to fill your tank is to put in an old plate or saucer and pour the water onto it to prevent churning up the sand or gravel. Fill the tank a third or half full, and then put in the plants. Poke their roots into the sand. They may tend to float up again, in which case you can weigh their roots down with small, well-scrubbed stones, either tied on with cotton or just placed on top. Bunch the plants together to give your fishy tenants somewhere to hide and make them feel at home. A tunnel of rocks is also good (providing they are fixed firmly and not likely to topple on to a passing fish). Add water to within two or three centimetres of the top.

By the way, do try to set the tank up where you will keep it, so you won't have to move it later. Water is incredibly heavy, and you won't want your tank to

98

spring a leak. The best place is where it is light enough for the plants to grow, but not in direct sunlight. This may be too hot for the fish and also encourage masses of green algae to grow on the tank sides. Algae is, of course, not harmful to the fish. In fact, they often pick at it when it is especially furry, but it will mean that you can't see the fish too well. If algae *does* become a problem, you can buy a special holder from the aquarium shop for a razor blade (be careful not to cut yourself, though), and scrape the sides of the tank down.

Put a cover (glass or plastic, providing it is raised, or perforated zinc) on the tank in case an enterprising fish tries to jump out. Leave the whole tank to settle for a week until the water clears and the bubbles have gone.

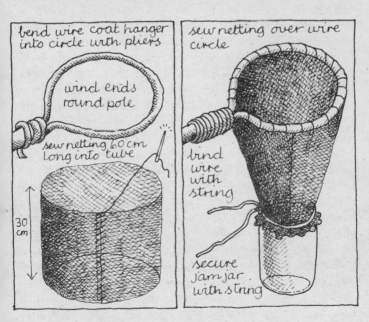

How to make a pond net

Now – and only now – catch your fish! Only take a very few (partly not to upset the balance of nature in your locality, and partly so you don't overcrowd them, which often has disastrous results). A useful 'rule-of-thumb' formula for keeping fish is a centimetre of fish body length (not including the tail) to 60 square centimetres of water surface.

Use a net to catch your fish. You can make one as shown in the illustration on page 99. Don't use a hook and line, as this will damage the fish. Take with you a large jam jar or fish can with cover to carry them home. Do get home as quickly as you can and try not to jolt them, so they will have the best chance of survival.

Many fish from the wild don't do too well in aquaria, but young specimens of the species mentioned should be all right. Sticklebacks are very inclined to terrorise smaller fish, and keep a tank in a constant state of panic. Either keep only young ones, or one adult pair which you hope will breed. In a 60 cm aquarium, sticklebacks do very well, are very active and may well breed. Then you will have all the fun of watching the male build the nest, drive the female into it and then himself rear the babies! He's no male chauvinist, the stickleback!

Unfortunately, sticklebacks shouldn't be fed on packet fish foods, but you can give them daphnia or micro-worms (see Chapter 19). Occasionally, they'll also take bits of dried liver. Minnows will take fine breadcrumbs, and daphnia (water fleas) from a pet shop, and some bigger fish will eat those ant pupae wrongly described as 'ant's eggs'. Feed the fish once a day. Take away any food uneaten after half an hour. Whatever you do, don't overfeed them, or they will surely die because they just go on and on eating until they are bloated. When I was a child, a helpful elderly neighbour looked after my tropical fish while I was away

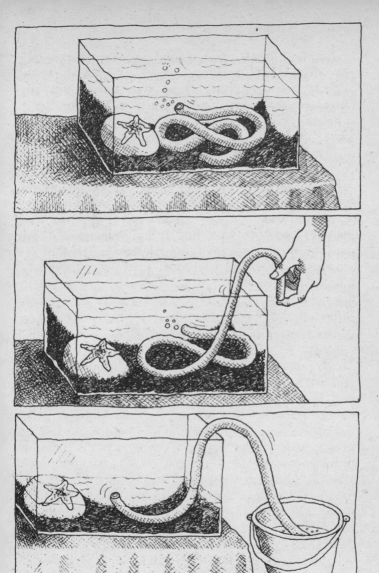

How to siphon

on holiday. Thinking she was doing them a favour, she gave them double rations – for a fortnight! The result was that when I got back, over half of the tank's inhabitants were floating gruesomely upside down on top of the tank – very, very dead! After that, whenever I went away, I left the fish unfed. They won't starve for a couple of weeks and they will clean up the tank most beautifully.

While on the subject of cleaning, you must, of course, normally keep the tank clean yourself, by siphoning out bits of refuse, fish droppings, etc. Include some water snails and they will eagerly help keep the tank clean by scavenging the debris. Look at the drawings on page 101 for how to do this.

16

Keeping sea creatures

You *can* with great care keep some sea creatures, but this is *much* more tricky than keeping freshwater animals. The vital thing to remember is that sea creatures absolutely *must* have sea water to live in – *and* you will have to change it frequently. So, either you have to live near the sea where you can get the water easily, or you have to make it artificially from one of the variety of powders in pet shops (all needing quite complicated mixing). After reading so far, you may quite sensibly decide keeping sea creatures is just too difficult for you, and settle for something less demanding.

If, after considering it carefully, you decide to have a go, you should set up a shallow aquarium (a white plastic bowl is good) with your sea water and clean sea sand on the bottom. Provide some stones as hidey-holes. These should be from the seashore and may be ones on which barnacles, tubeworms and anemones are living. Add some green or red seaweeds. Don't use brown ones as they will go slimy and smell. The red and the green seaweeds will help aerate the water by releasing oxygen during the daytime. (You really should aerate the tank with an electrically driven air pump – from an aquarist's shop – if you are going to keep most sea creatures more than a day or so, although hermit crabs and prawns are all right without. If you don't use an aerator, you must empty and fill the tank with fresh seawater every day, preferably with a siphon (look at the picture on page 101). Keep your aquarium as cool as possible and out of bright sunlight. Cover with perforated zinc to stop crabs, etc, clambering out.

Generally, remember to collect only a very few, small creatures. The best animals to keep are crabs, prawns, shrimps and sea anemones. Don't try to keep fish as they seldom survive the journey home. If, like barnacles and anemones, the creatures are attached to a rock, bring a piece of the rock home as well. Carry everything home in a bucket of *sea* water. Most creatures other than the ones mentioned above should be kept for only a few hours, just long enough to study them, and then taken back to the sea. Sea snails are hard to keep. Not only do they need sea water but the food they eat is usually in the sea.

Carnivorous beasts such as crabs will eat small bits of white raw fish (a quarter of a centimetre square), or tubifex or microworms. Herbivores will eat seaweeds. Mussels, barnacles and tubeworms filter particles of food from the water. Always feed each herbivorous beast in turn, putting the food on the end of long plastic forceps. If you don't have these, there are some joined salad servers which would do as well. Make sure when feeding them that you never leave pieces of food in for long, as they will foul the water. An hour is quite long enough. Also remember to remove any dead animals.

Sea creatures not too difficult to keep are prawns and hermit crabs. Both will eat minced up cooked meat (raw meat would foul the tank). As hermit crabs are very untidy eaters, it may be better to put them *and* their food for an hour each day in a separate dining tank filled with sea water. As for prawns, hook or siphon out any food they haven't eaten after an hour. Don't overfeed your marine pets. In fact, underfeeding is always better than overfeeding which may kill them.

When you go prawning, take a prawning net. Prawns are quite nippy. Remember they walk *forwards* but swim *backwards*. For sea creatures, they are quite hardy, but it's best only to keep about six small specimens at a time. Change their water frequently, as soon as (and preferably before) bubbles stay on the surface when you stir the water. It's better to change a little water each day, rather than change the whole lot at one fell swoop. Make sure the water you add is a similar temperature to the old water. You can achieve this by floating the new water in a polythene bag in the old water for 20 minutes or so, before putting it in. The water level for both prawns and crabs should be quite shallow, about 15 to 20 cm.

Collect hermit crabs at low tide among the seaweeds and rocks. Give them some empty whelk or similar shells about the same size as themselves. Hermit crabs have no inbuilt hard shells. They have to squat in empty shells of other creatures such as whelks. As the crabs grow, they need bigger and better housing. They are good fun to watch while they go house-hunting. They try out several empty shells for size, until they find one that suits them. But they seem never to be satisfied and are constantly moving house. The more empty shells you give them, the more frequently they will change their homes.

17

Rescuing victims from the cat

However fond people are of cats, few like their habit of torturing birds, mice, voles and other small creatures. It is, of course, a cat's instinct to catch and play with such small creatures, and there are times when this is very useful. Many government departments have a number of cats on their payroll. They're called rodent operatives and are 'paid' in catfood. Equally useful are farm and other working cats whose 'job' is to catch or deter rats and mice in barns and haystacks, factories, offices and dockyards.

But one day your own pet moggy bounces in through his cat flap and, with an immense air of pride, drops at your feet a live baby field mouse, a fledgling bird, a tiny vole or shrew. However strongly other people – and maybe yourself – proclaim it's only nature, sometimes it's very difficult to let nature take its course and leave the poor victim to its fate.

Here are a few hints on how to help and, if you can manage to rescue it alive and unmangled, how to keep the victim just long enough to let it recover.

Step number one – how to get it away from a very pleased and possessive cat. This is a real problem. First – catch your cat! Easier said than done, if he thinks you may rob him of his rightful prey. I find with my cat that the best course (though not always successful) is not to yell at him nor scold. He'll only run off with the prey, and in any case you should never shout at animals – it only confuses them. Walk quietly up to him, perhaps saying neutrally, 'What have you got there then?' and then *grab* him firmly! Then *you've* got him, and *he's* got the mouse! Take them both outside so that, if the victim is basically unharmed, he can scurry away as soon as he is released from the cat's jaws.

If you then squeeze the cat quite hard, he will probably open his mouth to protest and so drop his catch. (This may sound a bit unkind, but I don't think it hurts or damages him, and it's not for long.) Of course, if your cat's very cussed, he may refuse to drop the prey, and give it a final scrunch to prevent you taking it from him. Well, it sounds heartless, but as least this will finish the mouse or bird off quickly and spare him the minutes of torture while Puss plays with him.

Having released the prey, shut the cat up for half an hour or so in a shed or garage – not indoors if he has a cat flap, or he'll shoot straight out again and probably pounce on the mouse again.

Now you can turn your attention to the sufferer. If it's a mouse or similar rodent, and not too hurt to run, he may have shot into a dark corner, and you may have difficulty in finding him. Do locate him if you can, as he may be suffering in a quiet spot and could die in lengthy agony, unless you put him out of his misery.

Having tracked down your mouse, see how badly wounded he is – if at all. Sometimes this is difficult to assess because the injuries may be internal and not show. If you have an injured bird, take him to the nearest vet, or animal clinic such as the PDSA. Only if there are very special reasons why you can't do this should *you* try to treat a bird.

If a small rodent has obvious large wounds and is bleeding badly, there's not really much you can do for him. He'll probably die anyway – and any nursing you do will just prolong his suffering. So screw up your courage, get a heavy piece of wood or metal (gruesome as it sounds, I find a wooden mallet is very effective and doesn't mangle the animal too much). Give him a quick, sharp blow, and his suffering is over. Then you can bury him in a quiet corner of the garden.

If you're not too sure how injured the victim is, or he doesn't appear to be wounded in any way, always give him the benefit of the doubt before bonking him on the head. He may just be suffering from shock (and a *huge* human hovering over him isn't going to help him get over it!). So give him some hospital treatment for a little while.

I use an old aquarium as a hospital ward – without water, of course, and with a glass lid raised a centimetre from the top for air. However, a small shoe box or other suitable container will do just as well. Put some newspaper in the bottom to soak up any mess, and a bit of hay, wood shavings or torn-up paper for comfort. Add a shallow dish of suitable food (breakfast cereal is usually handy) and another shallow dish or tin lid of water. Pick the creature up carefully, pop him in and leave him alone for half an hour or so in a warm place (near the kitchen boiler is a good spot). After a little while peep at him – from a distance. If he's really hurt, he'll probably be still lying motionless, perhaps on his side. If then you think he's unlikely to recover, it's kinder to put him out of his misery.

If, however, he looks as if he might be reviving, give him longer, but *do* leave him in peace. Probably more animals die from shock than injuries – and he is probably much more terrified of you than of the cat!

Don't pick him up again, stroke him or touch him. When you're really ill in bed, you want to be left alone, don't you, even when you know your visitors. The mouse cannot understand you're trying to help him. He only knows you're HUGE, and strange, and terrifying!

If he's still alive the next day and fairly lively, then let him go. If he seems all right but a bit sluggish, try keeping him another day. By the way, if the victim is a mouse or other small rodent, he will begin to gnaw his way out of the box as soon as he recovers – so do check on him periodically. They can even escape from a tank. The glass cover to my hospital tank has a small corner broken off, and more than one patient has climbed the 20 cm or more of the vertical glass tank side, wriggled through the hole and done a moonlight flit. Another one nibbled his way through a muslin cover about a foot above his head! It is a wonder my house and garage are not overrun with field mice. I like to think that such a lively Houdini must have been fit and well to escape so cleverly.

People often want to help not only bird-victims of cats, but also young or exhausted birds they may come across. If the bird is a young one, make sure it really does need help. Lots of fledglings leave the nest and hang around waiting to be fed, before they can really fly. Leave the parents to sort them out – they really *don't* need rescuing!

If the bird is fully grown and you can pick it up, it definitely is sick and needs help. If it seems not to be injured, but just exhausted or starving, put it in your hospital box. The box should be fixed up as for mammals, but with a perch stick jammed low across the box. Put an opaque cover on as birds tend to fly up to the light and may injure themselves against a glass lid. Seed-eaters will eat budgie mixture, and insect-eaters live insects and chopped worms. If at first you can't get the right food (in my experience casualties always seem to happen after shop-closing hours on a Saturday), a little soaked bread will do, but don't give them alcohol. Leaving a light on for a few hours will encourage a bird to feed. As mentioned before, wounded birds should go straight to the nearest vet or animal clinic and, if possible, you should ring first. (Look for the number in Yellow Pages.)

Once the bird is well enough, you must let it go. It is in any case illegal to keep wild birds, as well as being very unkind. Remember it is also illegal to collect eggs or young birds from the nest. You are only allowed to kill it humanely if it is obviously too badly injured to recover even if taken to the vet.

Let us assume your bird has recovered. Take it outside and let it go. You will probably feel rather miserable when it flies away, but you should feel pleased that you've done such a good job in helping it back to its natural life.

You can also release your field mice and voles, well away from any house, once they are well enough. One hint: many people do not feel as sympathetic to mice and other rodents as you do. They may well have fifty fits if you announce you've let a mouse go (instead of killing it, as they would have done). So, it's as well to be discreet. Don't announce your achievement to the world unless you're sure those around you are wildlife lovers too!

18

Liberty pets

As well as the creepy crawly pets described in this book, and the more traditional domestic pets (cats, dogs, rabbits, guinea pigs, gerbils and so on), with patience you can make pets of a kind from some of the wild creatures that visit your garden. Some will, of course, become tamer than others, but you can still have a lot of fun and interest from pets in your garden (hedgehogs, toads, squirrels, birds, etc). You must never forget though that they are wild creatures whose rightful home and habitat is the wild.

Hedgehogs are fascinating animals. The best time to see them is in the early evening, or after rain when they are slug-and-snail hunting. Because they adore eating such garden pests they are popular with gardeners. Hedgehogs can be tamed quite easily. If you put out a dish of bread-and-milk regularly for a hedgehog, he will soon learn it's there, and even rattle the empty dish to remind you if you forget. This is a point to remember when feeding wild creatures. You must be regular in feeding them as they come to rely on it.

If you move quietly, once the hedgehog gets used to you, he won't roll up into a ball. But take care if you pick him up. It is best to wear a pair of gardening gloves. Hedgehogs tend to be infested with fleas and other parasites. I have heard (but never tried it myself) of people offering a hedgehog a home. A wooden box with one end open, and leaves and dry grass inside for bedding, makes an inviting house. If you try this, put your bread-and-milk, plus some fruit, vegetable, meat and worms, near it, and with luck you may find the hedgehog uses it. Don't forget that hedgehogs hibernate and that they will often choose a garden dump to sleep in, so do rake over your bonfire before lighting it – or a hedgehog will meet a very nasty end.

On spring and summer evenings you may hear strange grunting noises in the garden. If you follow them up, you may be lucky enough to see two courting hedgehogs endlessly circling each other. Later on, you may discover their nest full of baby hedgehogs. Watch them carefully from a distance, and take care not to disturb them. I once had a hedgehog nest for a number of years in some thick undergrowth against the wall of my house, and had great fun watching the babies. One year, to my horror, the mother hedgehog got entangled in the fruit cage netting and by the time she was discovered she seemed to have been there for several hours. We hastily cut her free (she was completely entwined) and took her back to her family. They were *very* hungry (hedgehogs are mammals and feed on their mother's milk) and greeted her with squeals of delight.

Hedgehogs are useful to the gardener but grey squirrels are quite the opposite, gnawing bark from live trees and chewing young shoots. Squirrels are not popular with farmers and tree growers and, as they have a nasty bite, it's not a good idea to get near them. But they can be good fun to watch from a distance in your garden. One that visits my garden wraps his tail around a branch, reinforces it with his back feet and uses his front paws to haul up nuts left for the birds.

Putting coconuts in the garden is a great way to encourage birds like tits to your garden, and a wide variety of birds will come if you offer several types of food. Loose food should be placed on a bird table built to deter cats. If you just scatter the food on the ground, a moggy may lie in wait for the birds who come to feed. Look at the picture, on page 114, of how to make a simple bird table. Good sorts of food to put on it are

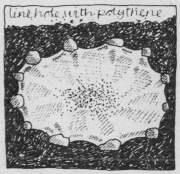

How to make a bird bath

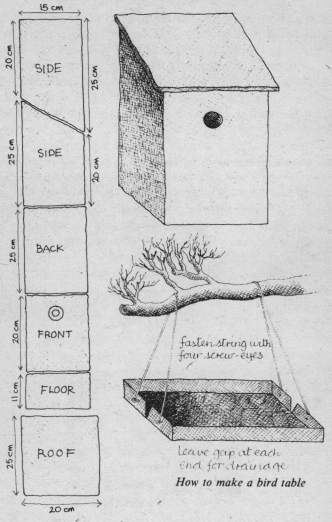

15 cm

20 cm

SIDE

25 cm

SIDE

25 cm

25 cm

20 cm

BACK

FRONT

11 cm

FLOOR

25 cm

ROOF

20 cm

How to make a nesting box

fasten string with
four screw-eyes

Leave gap at each
end for drainage

How to make a bird table

birdseed, brown breadcrumbs, pieces of fat, etc. You can also hang half a fresh coconut, a string of peanuts or a piece of fat from the meat joint below it or from a tree branch. But never offer salted peanuts or desiccated coconut.

A bird bell is fun to make too. Fill an old yoghurt pot with pieces of kitchen scraps, seed, bread, nuts, etc, and pack it all in with some melted bacon or other fat. Insert a loop of string into the fat before it sets. Then carefully ease it out of the pot and hang it up for the tits. Remember again, if you feed birds regularly they will come to rely on it, so, especially in winter, you must not stop or they may die. In winter, too, birds often die from thirst rather than hunger, so a bird bath, made from an old dustbin lid or a piece of polythene laid in a pit, is good for them. Keep the water free from ice.

You could also make, perhaps with a bit of help, a nesting box. Always hang a nesting box facing north, and be prepared to leave it there even for several years before any bird approves of your choice of home for it. If you are lucky and birds do occupy it, curb your impatience and do not disturb the parents by peeping in or they may desert the nest. Of course, you should never take any of the eggs – or any eggs from any nest. This is not only illegal, but might contribute to making a species of bird extinct. Look at the pictures showing how to make a bird nesting box and a bird table.

Very, very rarely (sometimes never in your whole life) you may find a baby animal such as a young rabbit or fox cub abandoned for some reason by its mother, or orphaned through an accident or a shooting party. If a fox cub is very tiny, you can rear it like a puppy, giving it the same food, especially raw meat. And you can train it to a lead like a puppy. Quite recently, I saw a fox cub only a few weeks old in a pub bar, contentedly sitting on the end of a lead and obviously enjoying being stroked and petted. But if you have to take on such a task, it's as well to get as much help and advice as you can from a vet or other animal-lover. Remember, too, that a wild creature may always want to return to the wild – but that it will not have learned to hunt for its own food and could starve if set free suddenly. You should seek advice from a wildlife expert on how to help your pet adjust to the wild state.

Baby rabbits are very tricky to feed. Ask your vet for help. You will have to feed your rabbit many times a day, through a dropper, for several weeks until he can eat normal rabbit food. You may feel such a responsibility is just too much. In which case don't abandon the little creature to die – it's much kinder to have him painlessly put down by the vet.

If you happen to have a cat with very young kittens when you find your rabbit, it may be possible to persuade her to adopt him. Wait until the mother cat has left her family to go out for a while and then pop the rabbit among the kittens. This will ensure that the kittens' smell transfers to the foundling. Watch the cat carefully when she returns home, in case she recognizes the newcomer for what he could become – a potential dinner! The chances are that she will give him a quick lick as she does to all her babies and will curl up contentedly around her increased family. The rabbit will probably need help to find and feed from the cat's teats, but once he's got the idea he should be well away. He will, however, grow up quicker than the plump and waddling kittens and perplex his foster mother by leaping out of the box and scampering around the floor. Naturally she will hop out after this precocious child to retrieve him by the scruff of the neck. Don't be alarmed! This is the way cats – and dogs – normally

116

carry their young, and having once accepted your rabbit as a foster child she isn't going to eat him. Remember to offer your herbivorous baby proper rabbit food as well as soon as he is hopping around.

19

Breeding live food

In winter it can be quite difficult – or expensive – to get supplies of live food for those pets that need it. It's not difficult, however, to breed it yourself. Items you can supply quite easily are maggots called gentles (which, after a chrysalis stage, turn into blowflies), mealworms (larvae of a beetle that lives in cereals like bran), and fruit flies. For water pets you can also provide daphnia, micro-worms (white worms) and infusoria.

Gentles
Buy some from an angling shop (anglers use them as bait). Feed some immediatly to your pets, and put the rest into two containers. Jam jars, providing they have securely fastened lids with small airholes in, are fine. Or you could use a plastic sandwich box with some sawdust in it. Put one container in a warm place so the gentles start their metamorphosis quite quickly. Eventually, after the pupa stage, blowflies will emerge. Hence the need for secure lids! Do make *absolutely sure* they cannot get out as they are notorious kitchen pests and do carry germs to food. If you give them a piece of meat they will lay eggs on it from which the gentles will hatch, and in this way you have an endless supply of gentles.

The second container of gentles goes into a cooler place so they develop more slowly. When you have finished with the first container, you move the second one into the warmer place. By continually recycling them you can have constant supplies of either gentles or blowflies, depending on what your pets need. (Incidentally, if you keep the pupae dormant at a temperature of about 40 degrees Fahrenheit, 5 degrees Centigrade, you can regulate when they hatch.)

Mealworms

Buy a few mealworms from a pet shop. Fill a biscuit or cake tin or plastic container with alternating layers of paper, corrugated cardboard or rags, and a mixture of bran and breadcrumbs, crumbled biscuits and some vegetable peelings (potato or carrot). Put a few mealworms in each layer. Put on a lid punched with a few small holes.

Within two weeks, most of the mealworms will have become pupae which will eventually hatch into beetles. Neither stages are much good as food, but from them you will get an endless supply of mealworms. The colony can go on for at least a year. All you have to do is add more food from time to time and keep the colony at a temperature between 25 and 30 degrees Centigrade. (Your family may be relieved that mealworm culture is very clean and smell-free!)

Fruit flies

These are small flies often found hovering over rotting fruit. Just put a 2 to 3 cm thick paste of brown bread, banana and water on the bottom of a jar – and stand back! Trap half a dozen of them, and put them in a large jar with some food and cover the jar firmly with gauze and a rubber band. After five days you will obtain a large number of other flies, and five jars started at daily intervals will give you an endless supply, since their breeding cycle is five days!

Micro-worms (white worms)
These are very good for feeding to fish and other water creatures. Buy a starter supply from the pet shop or aquarist. Put them on soil in an old seedbox with a mixture of bread and milk or oatmeal on the surface. Keep covered with a sheet of glass in contact with the soil and put damp sacking over the glass.

Daphnia (waterfleas)
It's best to start off with some from a pet shop. You can breed them by putting them in a large container, such as an old sink. Feed by scattering dried ox blood obtainable from a pet shop on the surface of the water. Skim them off with a fine net when your pets need a snack.

Infusoria soup
There are two main ways of breeding this food which is very useful for fish fry and small aquarium creatures.

Method 1
Put some water from an aquarium into a jam jar. Bruise some fresh lettuce leaves and float them on the water. Put the whole thing into a warm, dark cupboard (the ever-useful airing cupboard, perhaps, if you can get permission). After three days, you will see a faint white cloud in the water, which is in fact a swarm of tiny creatures. A spoonful is sufficient for about 50 fry.

After a few days the water gets very foul and needs to be thrown away, so it is best to start a fresh jar every couple of days and then you can have a constant supply of infusoria soup.

Method 2
A spare tank or old sink in the garden, filled with water from an aquarium in use for some time. Carry on with the lettuce leaves etc as in Method 1. Every time you take out a jar of the 'soup', replace with a jar of tap water. This prevents the 'pong' in the house, but does mean the tank may get pests which could be harmful to your pets.

Addresses

Museums

British Museum (Natural History), especially Departments of Entomology and Herpetology, Cromwell Road, London, SW1.

Bristol Museum, Queen's Road, Bristol 8

Liverpool Museum, Merseyside County Museums, William Brown Street, Liverpool 3

Exeter Museum, Rougemont House Museum, Castle Street

Cardiff Museum, Civic Centre, Cardiff

Edinburgh Museum, Chambers Street, Edinburgh EH1 1JF

Societies

The Amateur Entomological Society, 1 West Ham Lane, London, E15

The Royal Entomological Society, 41 Queens Gate, London, SW7

The British Herpetological Society, c/o Zoological Society of Great Britain, London, NW1

The Freshwater Biological Association, The Ferry House, Ambleside, Westmorland

The Royal Society for the Protection of Birds, Sandy, Bedfordshire (has a Junior Branch)

Also, there are many local entomological, herpetological and general natural history societies. Contact your local museum or library, or the Town Council.

Some zoos have clubs for young naturalists, eg the XYZ Club of the London Zoo, Regents Park, London, NW1

Other useful addresses
The Butterfly Farm, Billington, Ashford, Kent
Worldwide Butterflies Ltd, Brighton and Lyme Regis (butterflies, equipment and books)
Worldwide Butterflies Ltd, Over Compton, Sherborne, Dorset (butterfly farm) can sometimes supply silkworm eggs

Useful books to read

Observer's books: *Butterflies, Caterpillars* etc. Warne
A Field Guide to the Butterflies of Britain and Europe,
  Higgins and Riley, Collins
*A Field Guide to the Insects of Britain and Northern
  Europe,* Chinery, Collins
*Grasshoppers, Crickets and Cockroaches of the British
  Isles,* Ragge, Warne
Butterflies, Goodden, Hamlyn All-Colour Paperback
The Oxford Book of Insects, Burton, OUP
The Freshwater Life of the British Isles, Clegg, Warne
How to Begin the Study of Entomology, Wootton,
  British Naturalist Association pamphlet
Crickets and Grasshoppers of the British Isles, Haes,
  British Naturalist Association pamphlet
Insects and their World, Oldroyd, British Museum
Pleasure from Insects, Tweedie, David and Charles
Studying Insects: A Practical Guide, Ford, Warne
Create a Butterfly Garden, Newman, Baker
Pond and Stream Life, Clegg (ed), Blandford
Caterpillars of the British Butterflies and Moths, Stokoe
  and Stoven, Warne
Insects are Animals, Too, Wootton, David and Charles
Keeping Unusual Pets, Miller, Studio Vista
A Silkworm is Born, Stepp, Sterling Nature Series/Oak
  Tree Press

The Insects in your Garden, Oldroyd, Kestrel/Puffin

Let's look at Spiders, Smith, Hart Davis

Tortoises, Lizards and other Reptiles, Le Roi, Nicholas Vane

Nest Boxes, British Trust for Ornithology, Beech House, Tring, Herts

Keeping Reptiles and Amphibians, Leutscher, David and Charles

Keeping Spiders, Insects and other Land Invertebrates, Frances Murphy, Bartholomew